Daniel:
Breathtaking

Word of His Mouth Publishers
Mooresboro, NC

All Scripture quotations are taken from the **King James Version** of the Bible.

ISBN: 978-0-9856042-6-4
Printed in the United States of America
©2013 Dr. Bo Wagner (Robert Arthur Wagner)
(Second Printing)

Word of His Mouth Publishers
PO Box 256
Mooresboro, NC 28114
704-477-5439
www.wordofhismouth.com

Table of Content

Dedication

Daniel started off as a young man living for the Lord and ended up as an old man living for the Lord. In between that start and that end, he lived a life of adventure, intrigue, faith, and excitement. It was not always easy; in fact, sometimes it must have been heartbreaking. But through it all Daniel stayed true and ended up as a shining example of what it means to be a real child of God. This is what I desire for my own son. Caleb has been a joy, a blessing from God; I cannot imagine life without him. My desire for him is that he be like Daniel. I know that he can, and I believe that he will. This book is dedicated to him, my son, Caleb Cordell Wagner.

Chapter 1
Heartbreak

Daniel 1:1 *In the third year of the reign of Jehoiakim king of Judah came Nebuchadnezzar king of Babylon unto Jerusalem, and besieged it.* **2** *And the Lord gave Jehoiakim king of Judah into his hand, with part of the vessels of the house of God: which he carried into the land of Shinar to the house of his god; and he brought the vessels into the treasure house of his god.*

The majority of the people never believed that it could happen. America had been so strong for so long, that when a few courageous preachers stood and predicted that the Chinese would invade her and wipe her out as a nation, they were almost universally laughed at. Late night talk show hosts had a field day with them, newscasters called them "crazy fundamentalists," and military leaders proudly proclaimed that America was way too strong for it to happen. Even a lot of "respectable" preachers got into the act, preaching week after week that America was God's golden child and would never fall to another nation.

The first hint of trouble came when all of our surveillance satellites mysteriously went down. What only a few people knew was that one military installation deep in the Arizona desert was controlling every one of them, and that the Chinese had managed to get a spy into a high rank in that very place. It took only a matter of a few minutes for the computer virus he installed to take effect, and all of the satellites went off-line simultaneously. No one knew that it was an inside job, our experts simply thought that a hacker had gotten a worm into the system, and that they would need a couple of days to fix things back up.

But at the very moment the satellites went down, all Hell began to break loose on America. The Chinese had spent years developing absolutely undetectable submarines, which were at that moment less than a hundred miles off of our western coast. Those subs were capable of firing cross-continental ballistic missiles, each one carrying low-yield nuclear warheads. All of our major military installations were completely destroyed before we even knew what was happening.

The Chinese had learned some things from the mistakes the Japanese made at Pearl Harbor three-quarters of a century before. They knew that the destruction must be swift and complete, with no chance for America to gather herself to fight back. With our military installations decimated in that very first attack, the Chinese moved quickly into the next stage of their plan. They went live with a world-wide news feed and claimed full responsibility for the attack. They then signaled their intention to destroy America forever and let it be known in no uncertain terms that any nation who moved to help us would face a full nuclear attack. The world blinked... and one by one the nations of the world let Beijing know that they would stay out of things.

Wave after wave of super ships began to stream for our shores, carrying tens of thousands of Chinese soldiers. Within a matter of days, they were storming our beaches, backed up by an air force larger than anyone ever dreamed they had. For years they had carefully stolen our technology, and now they were using planes and missiles and guns designed by our own engineers and scientists against us. America, so use to being protected by an ocean on either side of us, simply fell apart at the sight of enemy troops marching in our streets. Our liberal government had long since abolished the second amendment, so no citizen had any way to resist. Our schools and media had spent so many years sissifying our boys – not letting them keep score at sports so no one would get their feelings hurt, not letting them play dodge ball so no one would get bruised, teaching them "conflict resolution" instead of wrestling – that not many of them would have resisted if they could.

Everything really took less time and effort than the Chinese could have hoped. They were quickly approached for peace; Americans had gotten so squeamish at casualties, they figured peace at all costs was the way to go.

The cost was high. Every member of the United States military that was not killed in the initial and follow-up attacks was rounded up and slaughtered on world-wide television, just to send a message. Then, plans were announced to ensure that America would never rise again as a land. More than 90% of her 300,000,000 people were going to be taken captive to mainland China and forced to work as slaves. The only ones left behind would be the poorest and the least educated, people who could be easily handled.

The day that the last ship of captured Americans was deported, one last thing was in store. It took an incredible amount of work to do it, but every American flag on U.S. soil had been gathered into a mound the size of a small mountain, and placed in an empty field near the dock. As the last ship pulled away, a little child pointed back, smoke was rising. Tears began to stain every face, as the inferno grew. Miles out to sea, hours and hours later, the smoke was still visible, the only reminder of what was once a proud land, a land that would never ever be the same...

*   *   *   *   *

Hearing that story that all of us hope will never happen, you might feel just a little bit, just the tip of the iceberg of what the Jews felt so many years ago when they were conquered by

9

Babylon. What you would feel if this were real is like what they really felt, because for them, the horror was real. That is the entry emotion to the book of Daniel. There are not many things you can ever read that will make you gasp on each and every page. There is no letdown anywhere in this book. It is high octane, intense drama, terrifying fear, miraculous rescues, military conquests, divine interventions, and stunning prophecies all the way through it.

Daniel has both the old and the new. It looks back to what was, but also ahead to what will be. It is a companion book to the book of the Revelation. It is huge in its scope, but it also will draw you in. You see, this isn't just the story of world powers, it is the story of world powers as seen from the eyes of three or four people who were there and lived through it. You will not just get to know "things" through this book, you will also get to know some very interesting people. And through it all, on every single page, you are going to find things that will help you right now, today, tomorrow, every day for the rest of your lives.

The Sin

Deuteronomy 6:10 *And it shall be, when the LORD thy God shall have brought thee into the land which he sware unto thy fathers, to Abraham, to Isaac, and to Jacob, to give thee great and goodly cities, which thou buildedst not,* **11** *And houses full of all good things, which thou filledst not, and wells digged, which thou diggedst not, vineyards and olive trees, which thou plantedst not; when thou shalt have eaten and be full;* **12** *Then beware lest thou forget the LORD, which brought thee forth out of the land of Egypt, from the house of bondage.* **13** *Thou shalt fear the LORD thy God, and serve him, and shalt swear by his name.* **14** *Ye shall not go after other gods, of the gods of the people which are round about you;* **15** *(For the LORD thy God is a jealous God among you) lest the anger of the LORD thy God be kindled against thee, and destroy thee from off the face of the earth.*

When God spoke these words to Israel, Babylon was pretty much a non-entity, just a few back-of-the-desert nomadic tribesmen. Israel, on the other hand, was a nation on the rise. Hundreds of years earlier God had promised faithful Abraham, His friend, that He would make of him a great nation. Abraham had born Isaac, Isaac had born Jacob, and Jacob in turn had produced twelve sons. One of those sons, Joseph, was so hated by his brothers that they sold him as a slave into Egypt and then lied to their father about the entire affair, letting Jacob believe that his favorite son had been killed by wild beasts.

Years later, Godly and consistent Joseph had risen to the position of second in command of all the land of Egypt. He engineered Egypt's survival and the world's survival by saving up enough grain during seven good years to carry everyone through seven very bad years. Joseph's brothers, and then eventually his entire family, ended up down in Egypt with him. The brothers repented, Joseph forgave, and the family was restored.

But one day a new king arose over Egypt that did not know Joseph. The children of Israel became slaves in the land that Joseph had saved. Finally, God raised up Moses to deliver them from their bondage. A series of devastating plagues convinced Pharaoh to let them go. The Red Sea made sure that Egypt would not be a threat to them again.

After forty years of wandering caused by their own disobedience, the Israelites finally made it into the Promised Land. Joshua led the military conquest against all of the nations of Canaan.

This land that God gave them, Canaan, was described in glowing terms:

Great and goodly cities, which thou buildedst not, And houses full of all good things, which thou filledst not, and wells digged, which thou diggedst not, vineyards and olive trees, which thou plantedst not.

God gave them all of this on a silver platter! The walls of Jericho fell down flat, two alliances that the Canaanites put

11

together crumbled, the Gibeonites surrendered, God just rolled out the red carpet for them. And for all of this, God made one simple demand:

Ye shall not go after other gods, of the gods of the people which are round about you;

That was it. Just like in the Garden of Eden, one simple command, "Do not eat that one fruit." One command, "Stay away from those false gods." What could be easier? Why would anyone want to serve idols made of sticks and stones instead of the living God who made all things? But over and over and over again Israel went following after those same false gods: Baal, Moloch, Asherah, and so many others. This was the sin that God could not and would not tolerate from His covenant people.

God expects His people to have no allegiance to or even respect for false gods. And that is becoming a much bigger issue than you can imagine in our day. False gods are everywhere, and people from the church house, to the school house, to the media house, to the White House are opining that we need to have respect for them.

That is not the view of God. It never has been; it never will be. The god of Islam is a false god. The goddess of the Wiccans is a false god. The earth-god of the New Age movement is a false god. The god of Christian Science is a false god. The god of Buddhism is a false god. The hundreds of millions of gods of Hinduism are false gods. We are not to hold up as "respectable" something that claims to be God instead of God. We are certainly not to hold to or follow after those false gods. When Israel followed after false gods, she fell. And I am telling you now, as America forsakes the God of the Bible and holds up as respectable all of the false gods that the world has created, the hand of God will move from being for her to being against her. God has never tolerated idolatry, and He never will.

The Setting

Look at Daniel 1:1 again:

Daniel 1:1 *In the third year of the reign of Jehoiakim king of Judah came Nebuchadnezzar king of Babylon unto Jerusalem, and besieged it.*

Two kings and two kingdoms are spoken of in this verse. We will look at Nebuchadnezzar and Babylon shortly, but it is Judah and Jehoiakim that will give us the setting for what happened in Daniel 1:1.

Israel had begun her history as a nation as a Theocracy. Moses led her under God, then Joshua followed in that same path. Shortly after that she was ruled by a series of judges, who, in theory, were still promoting the Theocracy. But during the time of Samuel the Priest, Israel demanded to have her government changed from Theocracy (rule by the one true God) to monarchy (rule by a human king). When they would not take no for an answer, the days of the Jewish monarchy began under King Saul. He was tall, handsome, strong, and one of the worst things to ever happen to Israel. Self-willed and rebellious, set aside by God, he was then followed by David, a man after God's own heart. David was a great soldier... a great sinner... and a great sorrower.

After David came Solomon. Solomon brought the country to her greatest period of wealth and fame. And then at the height of it all, he made the most foolish decision imaginable:

1 Kings 11:1 *But king Solomon loved many strange women, together with the daughter of Pharaoh, women of the Moabites, Ammonites, Edomites, Zidonians, and Hittites;* **2** *Of the nations concerning which the LORD said unto the children of Israel, Ye shall not go in to them, neither shall they come in unto you: for surely they will turn away your heart after their gods: Solomon clave unto these in love.* **3** *And he had seven hundred wives, princesses, and three hundred concubines: and his wives turned away his heart.* **4** *For it came to pass, when Solomon was old, that his wives turned away his heart after other gods: and his heart was not perfect with the LORD his*

13

God, as was the heart of David his father. 5 For Solomon went after Ashtoreth the goddess of the Zidonians, and after Milcom the abomination of the Ammonites. 6 And Solomon did evil in the sight of the LORD, and went not fully after the LORD, as did David his father. 7 Then did Solomon build an high place for Chemosh, the abomination of Moab, in the hill that is before Jerusalem, and for Molech, the abomination of the children of Ammon. 8 And likewise did he for all his strange wives, which burnt incense and sacrificed unto their gods. 9 And the LORD was angry with Solomon, because his heart was turned from the LORD God of Israel, which had appeared unto him twice, 10 And had commanded him concerning this thing, that he should not go after other gods: but he kept not that which the LORD commanded. 11 Wherefore the LORD said unto Solomon, Forasmuch as this is done of thee, and thou hast not kept my covenant and my statutes, which I have commanded thee, I will surely rend the kingdom from thee, and will give it to thy servant. 12 Notwithstanding in thy days I will not do it for David thy father's sake: but I will rend it out of the hand of thy son.

If you marry wrong, you can expect it to be a multiple generation disaster. For Solomon, it was a disaster that eventually led to what happened in the first two verses of Daniel. Solomon's son, Rehoboam, caused a civil war. Ten tribes split away, becoming the Northern Kingdom that went by the name Israel. As history progressed that Northern Kingdom went through dozens of kings and every single one of them was wicked to the core. In 722 B.C. Israel fell captive to Assyria and never had a wholesale return.

But Judah, the Southern Kingdom, was better. Judah continued on for another 136 years, with a mixture of good kings and bad kings. All the while, though, she kept repeating the same mistakes the Northern Kingdom had made, following after idols instead of the one true God. Finally though, a man named Josiah came to the throne. Josiah was Jehoiakim's father. Josiah loved God. In a wicked and perverse nation, Josiah loved God and determined to serve him. Please, do not ever forget this: you can love and serve God no matter how wicked the world around you gets!

Josiah was eight years old when he became king. Talk about pressure! When he was twenty-six, something amazing and terrifying happened. He had commissioned some workers to fix up the Temple of God that had been desecrated. While those workers were at their job, they found something:

2 Kings 22:8a *And Hilkiah the high priest said unto Shaphan the scribe, I have found the book of the law in the house of the LORD...*

The fact that they "found" it means that it had been lost! For years, no one even looked at the Bible, because no one even knew where it was. What I find fascinating is that it was lost *in the house of God!* From what I can see, that is still happening a lot today. The Bible is being lost in the house of God. There are preachers telling people what "it should say" (in imaginary older and better manuscripts) instead of what it actually and simply says. When that happens, the Bible has been lost in the house of God. There are churches built around the idea of appealing to the lost world rather than pleasing God. When that happens, the Bible has been lost in the house of God.

Shaphan, the scribe, read the book of the law to the king, and when Josiah realized how badly his people had sinned through the years and how angry God was, he broke. He wept before God, repented, and led the nation in a revival. If only Josiah could have lived forever...

But there came a day when he interfered with a battle between two other nations, Egypt and Assyria, and needlessly lost his life. When he died, the last spark of hope for Judah died with him. Josiah's evil son Jehoahaz became king, but only for a little while (3 months) before he was carried away into Egypt. Then Josiah's son Eliakim was made king, and his name was changed to Jehoiakim, the same Jehoiakim of Daniel 1:1. Jehoiakim was as wicked and stubborn as his father had been righteous and humble, and God was done putting up with it.

The Siege

Daniel 1:1 *In the third year of the reign of Jehoiakim king of Judah came Nebuchadnezzar king of Babylon unto Jerusalem, and besieged it. 2 And the Lord gave Jehoiakim king of Judah into his hand, with part of the vessels of the house of God: which he carried into the land of Shinar to the house of his god; and he brought the vessels into the treasure house of his god.*

While Judah had been doing her dance with idolatry, 400 miles away, the Chaldeans, with their great capital city of Babylon, were quickly becoming the dominators of the world. That kingdom was started way back in Genesis 11 by Nimrod with the city and tower of Babel. In the last days of the kings of Judah, Babylon was ruled by Nabopollasser. But it was his famous son, Nebuchadnezzar, that defeated every remaining world power and made Babylon the terror of the earth. He defeated Pharaoh-necoh at Carchemish on the Euphrates in 605 B.C.[1] Nebuchadnezzar took the throne on 604 B.C. In the third year of Jehoiakim, Nebuchadnezzar finally got a little taste of what God had been dealing with in Judah and Israel's behavior. He actually had extended them some mercy through the years, and they basically slapped him in the face. So he finally decided that it was time to not be having any more trouble out of Judah. Two things happened, and we can find great application for our lives from these two things.

We first of all find that the king became a slave on his own throne. Nebuchadnezzar defeated the king of Judah and made him a "king under tribute." Basically, Jehoiakim was a slave on his own throne. He still wore the crown, he still lived in the royal city, but for eight more years he was a slave on his own throne. When you disobey God, you may still hold whatever position you have been in (father, mother, pastor, boss), but you will be nothing more than a slave on your own throne:

Romans 6:16 *Know ye not, that to whom ye yield yourselves servants to obey, his servants ye are to whom ye*

16

obey; whether of sin unto death, or of obedience unto righteousness?

It is bad to have a position and a title but no power behind it due to your own disobedience. Dad, mom, the position you have as parents is awesome, and it is normally very powerful. But when you disobey God, you will be a slave on your own throne; you will have the position without the power.

I will never forget the young lady from a seemingly good family who was rebelling. Her father was a student at the Bible College just three miles from my church, and they were attending my church at the time. Her parents brought her to the office to talk to my wife and myself so we could "help her come to terms with her rebellion." Dana and I spoke to her at length, but she would not so much as open her mouth: not a word, grunt, or syllable. Finally I said, "Young lady, I do not understand why you are like this, especially with such a Godly father..."

When I mentioned her "Godly father," the dam broke. She literally screamed at the top of her lungs, "You don't even know my daddy! My daddy is a hypocrite and a liar. He lives one way here at church for you to see and the exact opposite way at home! He smiles and shakes your hand every Sunday, Pastor, and then spends all week at home ripping you to shreds in front of us! Don't talk to me about my daddy; my daddy is a raving hypocrite and liar!"

When she left that day I told my wife, "There is nothing we can do to help her. Her wicked father has ruined her forever." Sure enough, she went on to become a drug addict, a drunk, and produced babies out of wedlock. Her parents' disobedience put them in a situation where they had the position of parents but without the power.

The second thing that happened when Israel disobeyed is that Judah's holy treasures became Babylon's souvenirs. Verse two says that many of the vessels of the house of God were taken from the house of God and brought into Babylon. This happened three different times, till there was not one thing

17

left. All of them ended up in the Temple of Bel, the false god of the Babylonians. Those vessels had been used through the years by the priests and high priests in the sacrifices to Jehovah God. They had helped in the shedding and sprinkling of the blood of lambs and in the washing of priestly hands. They were pure, sanctified, holy, and expensive vessels. They once meant something to Israel. They still meant something to God. Imagine what it was like when filthy Babylonian soldiers put their dirty, bloody hands out, grabbed those holy vessels, pawed all over them, and carried them to Babylon. Imagine the heartbreak of God and of Daniel, Hananiah, Azariah, and Mishael as those holy things were deposited in the Temple of Bel along with every sacrilegious thing imaginable. These were Israel's greatest treasures.

You can disobey God, but when you do, eventually your greatest treasures will be nothing more than souvenirs in the devil's hands. Disobey God sexually and your purity will become a souvenir in the devil's hands. Hang around the wrong crowd and your reputation will become a souvenir in the devil's hands. Drink booze and your once clear mind will become a souvenir in the devil's hands. Look at pornography and your marriage will become a souvenir in the devil's hands.

The only way to describe what happened in Daniel 1:1-2 is *Heartbreaking*. Unless a person is a total fool, he should be able to look at a mistake this big that Judah made, and he should be able to see the awful fallout. Seeing that, he should, if he has any sense, understand the fact that he does not have to do the same dumb things that Judah did. All along the way Judah made choices, and it was their own bad choices that led to the heartbreak. What kind of choices are you going to make, and what will they lead to?

Chapter 2
For Real

Daniel 1:3 *And the king spake unto Ashpenaz the master of his eunuchs, that he should bring certain of the children of Israel, and of the king's seed, and of the princes;* **4** *Children in whom was no blemish, but well favoured, and skilful in all wisdom, and cunning in knowledge, and understanding science, and such as had ability in them to stand in the king's palace, and whom they might teach the learning and the tongue of the Chaldeans.* **5** *And the king appointed them a daily provision of the king's meat, and of the wine which he drank: so nourishing them three years, that at the end thereof they might stand before the king.* **6** *Now among these were of the children of Judah, Daniel, Hananiah, Mishael, and Azariah:* **7** *Unto whom the prince of the eunuchs gave names: for he gave unto Daniel the name of Belteshazzar; and to Hananiah, of Shadrach; and to Mishael, of Meshach; and to Azariah, of Abednego.* **8** *But Daniel purposed in his heart that he would not defile himself with the portion of the king's meat, nor with the wine which he drank: therefore he requested of the prince of the eunuchs that he might not defile himself.* **9** *Now God had brought Daniel into favour and tender love with the prince of the eunuchs.* **10** *And the prince of the eunuchs said unto Daniel, I fear my lord the king, who hath appointed your meat and your drink: for why should he see your faces* *worse liking than the children which are of your sort? then shall ye make me endanger my head to the king.* **11** *Then said Daniel to Melzar, whom the prince of the eunuchs had set over Daniel, Hananiah, Mishael, and Azariah,* **12** *Prove thy servants, I beseech thee, ten days; and let them give us pulse to eat, and water to drink.* **13** *Then let our countenances be looked upon before thee, and the countenance of the children that eat of the portion of the king's meat: and as thou seest, deal with thy servants.* **14** *So he consented to them in this matter, and proved them ten days.* **15** *And at the end of ten days their countenances appeared fairer and fatter in flesh than all the children which did eat the portion of the king's meat.* **16** *Thus Melzar took away the portion of their meat, and the wine that they should drink; and gave them pulse.* **17** *As for these four children, God gave them knowledge and skill in all learning and wisdom: and Daniel had understanding in all visions and dreams.* **18** *Now at the end of the days that the king had said he should bring them in, then the prince of the eunuchs brought them in before Nebuchadnezzar.* **19** *And the king communed with them; and among them all was found none like Daniel, Hananiah, Mishael, and Azariah: therefore stood they before the king.* **20** *And in all matters of wisdom and understanding, that the king enquired of them, he found them ten times better than all the magicians and astrologers that were in all his realm.* **21** *And Daniel continued even unto the first year of king Cyrus.*

As we begin to delve deeply into the first chapter of the book of Daniel, I want to give you some introductory observations on these particular verses.

1.   The devil will seek out the best and brightest to steal from God and use for his own pleasure:
       Daniel 1:3 *And the king spake unto Ashpenaz the master of his eunuchs, that he should bring certain of the children of Israel, and of the king's seed, and of the princes;* **4a** *Children in whom was no blemish, but well*

favoured, and skilful in all wisdom, and cunning in knowledge, and understanding science, and such as had ability in them to stand in the king's palace,

These were not just average, run-of-the-mill young men that were taken into Babylon. These were the cream of the crop, the best and the brightest. The devil will take what he can get, but what he wants, what he targets, are the good ones. We make a mistake as parents and pastors when we assume that the devil is targeting the kid slouching on the back row, texting during service. The devil already has that one for now. The ones he really wants are the ones sitting up front, dressed right, with their Bibles open. If he can get those, he can do far more damage than he can by picking off the back-row boys and girls. Watch the good ones carefully, guard them with your lives; they are the ones the devil wants.

2.   The devil will try to re-train those best and brightest into his way of thinking:

Daniel 1:4b *and whom they might teach the learning and the tongue of the Chaldeans.*

This matter of indoctrination is important to the devil. His desire is to take church-raised, Godly young people and use all the means at his disposal to remove their Godly training and replace it with ungodly training. He will use public schools, and sadly, even some Christian ones. He will use Hollywood. He will use popular music. He will use social media. He will use colleges, which are, perhaps, his greatest tool since all of America worships at the altar of "higher education." Many good, young people have been twisted and warped by four years in a secular college away from home, away from the influence of mom and dad, away from the backing of a solid local church. Is secular college a sin? No, not necessarily. But, like dynamite, it can be either very helpful or completely destructive and needs to be handled with the greatest of care and preparation.

3.   The devil will try to change your diet:
        Daniel 1:5 *And the king appointed them a daily provision of the king's meat, and of the wine which he drank: so nourishing them three years, that at the end thereof they might stand before the king.*
        Having been fed a steady diet of right and truth, a child becomes a formidable force for the Lord. But if the devil can seduce a young person into a steady diet of entertainment, popular opinion, liberal ideology, and pleasure seeking, he can ruin that child.

4.   The devil will try to change your good name:
        Daniel 1:6 *Now among these were of the children of Judah, Daniel, Hananiah, Mishael, and Azariah:* **7** *Unto whom the prince of the eunuchs gave names: for he gave unto Daniel the name of Belteshazzar; and to Hananiah, of Shadrach; and to Mishael, of Meshach; and to Azariah, of Abednego.*
        It was common practice for a conquering nation to change the names of those prisoners that they desired to retrain for use in the royal court. In each case, the name change would not be a random thing. Whereas our American names usually have little or no

intrinsic meaning behind them, names in oriental cultures had specific and well-known meaning.

The names set aside and the new names assigned had great meaning in the case of these four boys. Daniel meant "God is my judge," Hananiah meant "God has favored," Mishael meant "Who is what God is?" and Azariah meant "Jehovah has helped." All of these names pointed clearly to the God of the Hebrews. Daniel had his name changed to Belteshazzar, which means "Bel's prince." Shadrach means "Inspired by the sun-god." Meshach means "Who is like (the goddess) Shak?" Abednego means "Servant of Nego." All of these new names reflected Chaldean deities.

Many years before this time, King Solomon uttered these words:

Proverbs 22:1 *A good name is rather to be chosen than great riches, and loving favour rather than silver and gold.*

These boys were not able to avoid having their names changed, but they were able to "maintain a good name!" These boys did not falter through any of these attacks. They were absolutely genuine, they were the real deal. That which is real is precious both to God and man.

Pick something, a diamond, a gold necklace, an antique, an autograph. In each case you will find that the real is precious, but the fake is not. Many replica Shelby Cobra cars have been sold through the years. But recently, the last remaining, *genuine*, specially built Shelby Cobra was sold. For $5.5 million!

That which is genuine is precious to man. That which is genuine spiritually is precious to God. If you are for real, you are precious to God. So what makes a Christian "For Real?" Let's work our way through the text and find out.

When your morality is not determined by your location, you are for real.

Daniel 1:3 *And the king spake unto Ashpenaz the master of his eunuchs, that he should bring certain of the children of Israel, and of the king's seed, and of the princes;*

They were in Babylon, not the hometown. The entire surrounding was wicked, and no parents were there to make them do right, yet they did right. So often, people's morality is determined by their location. For instance, they behave one way in church, but the opposite way somewhere else. One way around parents, the opposite way around friends. One way in front of the preacher and his wife, the opposite way when they are not around. One way in the "real world," another way online. There is a word for people whose morality changes with their location: hypocrites!

The story is told of a rather pompous-looking deacon who was endeavoring to impress upon a class of boys the importance of living the Christian life. "Why do people call me a Christian?" the man asked. After a moment's pause, one youngster who actually knew him said, "Maybe it's because they don't know you!"

I wonder, do people really know you? Are you the same "out there" as you are "in church?" If you are not, then you are not for real!

When you do right even when your greatest desires are taken from you, you are for real.

Daniel 1:4 *Children in whom was no blemish, but well favoured, and skilful in all wisdom, and cunning in knowledge, and understanding science, and such as had ability in them to stand in the king's palace, and whom they might teach the learning and the tongue of the Chaldeans.*

24

These boys are never recorded as getting married or having kids, and there is a very good reason why. The Babylonian practice was to make anyone near the throne a eunuch, so the king would never be at risk. Isaiah prophesied this very thing several years earlier while talking to King Hezekiah:

2 Kings 20:18 *And of thy sons that shall issue from thee, which thou shalt beget, shall they take away; and they shall be eunuchs in the palace of the king of Babylon.*

Talk about losing your greatest desires! Never able to marry, never able to have kids... I can predict what the vast majority of American Christians would do in the face of such loss: get bitter and stop serving God.

Many years ago I was in church with a man who confidently told us that God was going to heal his mother. When she died, he stopped serving God altogether.

Heartache is never easy, but it is part of this life. If heartache gets you to stop serving God, you are not for real. If you can only do right when the sun is shining and the soft breezes are blowing, you are not for real. But if you can experience heartbreak, cry your tears, go through your grief, and then go right back to serving God, you are for real.

When you make the right decisions in advance, and then stick to them no matter what the cost, you are for real.

Daniel 1:5 *And the king appointed them a daily provision of the king's meat, and of the wine which he drank: so nourishing them three years, that at the end thereof they might stand before the king.* **6** *Now among these were of the children of Judah, Daniel, Hananiah, Mishael, and Azariah:* **7** *Unto whom the prince of the eunuchs gave names: for he gave unto Daniel the name of Belteshazzar; and to Hananiah, of Shadrach; and to Mishael, of Meshach; and to Azariah, of Abednego.* **8** *But Daniel purposed in his heart that he would not defile himself with the portion of the king's meat, nor with the wine which he drank...*

25

This Hebrew word "purposed" means to fix, to establish, to constitute, to plant. Daniel knew that the law of God forbade the Jews from eating and drinking what the king was setting out. Daniel also knew that to not eat what the king was setting out could cost him his life. Daniel had already witnessed the brutality of the Babylonians during the siege of Jerusalem. He had seen people have their eyes gouged out, their heads cut off, and much worse. But Daniel and the boys determined to do right no matter what the cost!

The Bohemian reformer, John Hus, was a man who believed the Scriptures to be the infallible and supreme authority in all matters. He died at the stake for that belief in Constance, Germany, on his forty-second birthday. As he refused a final plea to renounce his faith, Hus's last words were, "What I taught with my lips, I seal with my blood."

Doing right may cost you a boyfriend or a girlfriend. Do right! Doing right may cost you money. Do right! Doing right may cost you a job. Do right! Do right, do right, do right, no matter what the cost! By the way, you will find that inevitably, not doing what is right will cost you more than if you had done right.

Some years ago, my wife was buying pool chemicals at a local business. A skunk had been hit by a car right out in front of the business, and the smell was overpowering. The business owner made the statement in my wife's hearing, "I would pay somebody $50.00 to get rid of that skunk for us!"

My wife said, "Do you mean that?"

He replied, "Sure!" So my wife called a man in our church that was out of work and told him about it. The young man drove down there, loaded up the smelly dead skunk, and hauled it off. But when he returned for his money, the owner would not pay him! He said, "The city would have come to get it eventually; I did not really need you to do that."

The young man called me on the spot, and I spoke to the business owner. I was pretty upset. The man said, "OK, look, just because I'm a good guy, I will give him $25.00." Then he hung up.

Two things happened after that. One, I paid the young man the other $25.00 out of my own pocket. Two, my wife and I never shopped there again! Every year we had spent hundreds of dollars with them, and all of that went away. But we also set about telling everyone else we knew not to shop with them. That business has lost multiplied thousands of dollars by not doing right.

When you determine to do right and then do it no matter what the cost, you are for real.

When your *disposition* is as good as your *position*, you are for real.

Daniel 1:8b *...therefore he **requested** of the prince of the eunuchs that he might not defile himself.*

Daniel knew he was in the right to not eat the king's meat or drink his wine. But look how politely he handled himself! I get the feeling Daniel was not around a whole lot of modern, "camp meetin' " preachers, otherwise he would have learned to be rude and mean while in the right. Listen to this quote from John Newton:

> *There is no right way to do a wrong thing. What will it profit a man if he gains his cause, and silences his adversary, if at the same time he loses that humble tender frame of spirit in which the Lord delights, and to which the promise of his presence is made!*

I saw a sign in a gas station some time back that put it another way: "You may be right, but if you're rude, you're wrong!" This goes from the pulpit to the pew: "You may be right, but if you're rude, you're wrong!" There is a preacher I know, way too well unfortunately. His doctrine is fine. But he is the most arrogant, hateful, prideful, caustic, mean-spirited excuse for a preacher I have met in a long time. No one but he and his are right, no one but he and his pray enough, no one but he and his win souls, no one but he and his handle God's money well enough, everyone is compromising, everyone needs to be preached against. He is a jerk!

27

That kind of thing is exactly why I take my church and my young people to only a few, well-chosen meetings. I have no use for rudeness from the pulpit. I have no use for preachers that cuss; I have no use for Christians who are haughty. I prefer to follow those who are Christ-like.

I love Daniel in this. He was right, but he was also polite. When your disposition is as good as your position, you are for real.

When you do not mind being put to the test, you are for real.

Daniel 1:9 *Now God had brought Daniel into favour and tender love with the prince of the eunuchs.* **10** *And the prince of the eunuchs said unto Daniel, I fear my lord the king, who hath appointed your meat and your drink: for why should he see your faces worse liking than the children which are of your sort? then shall ye make me endanger my head to the king.* **11** *Then said Daniel to Melzar, whom the prince of the eunuchs had set over Daniel, Hananiah, Mishael, and Azariah,* **12** *Prove thy servants, I beseech thee, ten days; and let them give us pulse to eat, and water to drink.* **13** *Then let our countenances be looked upon before thee, and the countenance of the children that eat of the portion of the king's meat: and as thou seest, deal with thy servants.*

We are living in the "how dare you question me" generation. People do not want to be examined; they do not want anyone checking them out. They want to tell people how they are and just have everyone believe them based on their word alone. But Daniel said, "Prove us." Put us to the test. Check us out, and you will know. If you are for real, you will be thrilled when people check you out.

In the early years of our church, a fine family (mom, dad, and six kids) showed up for a visit. They asked to speak to me after service. When we spoke, the father said, "Pastor, let me tell you why we are here. We heard several nasty things about your church from the local Bible College (he then told me every single one. If a tenth of them had been true, even I wouldn't have liked us!) and we decided that the only proper thing for us to do was to come check it out for ourselves. We have seen a good bit during the service, but we haven't had all of our questions answered yet. Would you mind if we asked you some questions?"

Without hesitation I said, "I don't mind a bit, ask away!" And they did. For an hour.

When they were done, he said, "I'm satisfied... how do we go about joining?" And join they did. And then a few years later, we had the privilege of sending them as missionaries out of our church to a foreign land. None of that would have happened if we had not been willing to be put to the test, willing to be checked out, willing to answer all questions!

I wonder, would you be nervous or upset if someone followed you around to see how you live? Why? Would you be nervous or upset if someone checked you out on Facebook or Myspace or other online sites? Why? Would you be upset if you were Googled? Why?

When you do not mind being put to the test, you are for real.

When you can be happy with the simple things in life, you are for real.

Daniel 1:12 *Prove thy servants, I beseech thee, ten days; and let them give us pulse to eat, and water to drink.* **13** *Then let our countenances be looked upon before thee, and the countenance of the children that eat of the portion of the king's meat: and as thou seest, deal with thy servants.* **14** *So he consented to them in this matter, and proved them ten days.* **15** *And at the end of ten days their countenances appeared fairer and fatter in flesh than all the children which did eat the portion of the king's meat.* **16** *Thus Melzar took away the portion of their meat, and the wine that they should drink; and gave them pulse.*

Pulse was basically "mashed up vegetables."

When my son was young, he learned a very valuable lesson about gratitude. He actually complained about a peach cobbler! A few days on vegetables and water made him a much more grateful child. If you have to have all the bells and whistles in life to make you happy, then you are nothing more than Paris Hilton minus the money. Look at the attitude that Paul had:

Philippians 4:11 *Not that I speak in respect of want: for I have learned, in whatsoever state I am, therewith to be content.* **12** *I know both how to be abased, and I know how to abound: every where and in all things I am instructed both to be full and to be hungry, both to abound and to suffer need.*

This world is not even home to us, we are just passing through! When you can live in modest means, with modest pleasures, you are getting close to the ideal of Scripture:

Philippians 4:5 *Let your moderation be known unto all men. The Lord is at hand.*

Jesus is coming soon, so why do we need all of the shiny things this world has to offer? When you can be happy with the simple things in life, you are for real.

When you live in such a way that you stand out from the world's crowd, you are for real.

Daniel 1:17 *As for these four children, God gave them knowledge and skill in all learning and wisdom: and Daniel had understanding in all visions and dreams.* **18** *Now at the end of the days that the king had said he should bring them in, then the prince of the eunuchs brought them in before Nebuchadnezzar.* **19** *And the king communed with them; and among them all was found none like Daniel, Hananiah, Mishael, and Azariah: therefore stood they before the king.* **20** *And in all matters of wisdom and understanding, that the king enquired of them, he found them ten times better than all the magicians and astrologers that were in all his realm.*

Historians tell us that there were a thousand or so young teens brought into Babylon at this time, including Daniel and his three friends. There were also all the multitudes of "magicians and astrologers" in Babylon! Yet Daniel and company stood out from them all. There truly was something special about them.

On the way back from a revival meeting some years ago, Dana and I got to laughing. We went down one short little street where just about every building was a "church!" The entire store front of the street looked like a religious mini-mall! When we stopped laughing, I told Dana, "I want to stand out. I don't want to settle for also-ran. I don't want to be another little church that folds after a few years." Individually, or as a body, here should be our attitude:

1 Corinthians 10:31 *Whether therefore ye eat, or drink, or whatsoever ye do, do all to the glory of God.*

Ecclesiastes 9:10a *Whatsoever thy hand findeth to do, do it with thy might...*

Colossians 3:23 *And whatsoever ye do, do it heartily, as to the Lord, and not unto men;*

Live right and do whatever you do excellently. Stand out from the world!

When what you have carries you on a straight path for an entire long lifetime, you are for real.

Daniel 1:21 *And Daniel continued even unto the first year of king Cyrus.*

Seventy plus years later, well into Daniel's late eighties or early nineties, he was still at it. He served God without a single known interruption his entire life! These men were real... and we should be too.

Chapter 3
Nightmare

Daniel 2:1 *And in the second year of the reign of Nebuchadnezzar Nebuchadnezzar dreamed dreams, wherewith his spirit was troubled, and his sleep brake from him.* **2** *Then the king commanded to call the magicians, and the astrologers, and the sorcerers, and the Chaldeans, for to shew the king his dreams. So they came and stood before the king.* **3** *And the king said unto them, I have dreamed a dream, and my spirit was troubled to know the dream.* **4** *Then spake the Chaldeans to the king in Syriack, O king, live for ever: tell thy servants the dream, and we will shew the interpretation.* **5** *The king answered and said to the Chaldeans, The thing is gone from me: if ye will not make known unto me the dream, with the interpretation thereof, ye shall be cut in pieces, and your houses shall be made a dunghill.* **6** *But if ye shew the dream, and the interpretation thereof, ye shall receive of me gifts and rewards and great honour: therefore shew me the dream, and the interpretation thereof.* **7** *They answered again and said, Let the king tell his servants the dream, and we will shew the interpretation of it.* **8** *The king answered and said, I know of certainty that ye would gain the time, because ye see the thing is gone from me.* **9** *But if ye will not make known unto me the dream, there is but one decree for you: for ye have prepared lying and corrupt words to speak before me, till the time be* *changed: therefore tell me the dream, and I shall know that ye can shew me the interpretation thereof.* **10** *The Chaldeans answered before the king, and said, There is not a man upon the earth that can shew the king's matter: therefore there is no king, lord, nor ruler, that asked such things at any magician, or astrologer, or Chaldean.* **11** *And it is a rare thing that the king requireth, and there is none other that can shew it before the king, except the gods, whose dwelling is not with flesh.* **12** *For this cause the king was angry and very furious, and commanded to destroy all the wise men of Babylon.* **13** *And the decree went forth that the wise men should be slain; and they sought Daniel and his fellows to be slain.* **14** *Then Daniel answered with counsel and wisdom to Arioch the captain of the king's guard, which was gone forth to slay the wise men of Babylon:* **15** *He answered and said to Arioch the king's captain, Why is the decree so hasty from the king? Then Arioch made the thing known to Daniel.* **16** *Then Daniel went in, and desired of the king that he would give him time, and that he would shew the king the interpretation.* **17** *Then Daniel went to his house, and made the thing known to Hananiah, Mishael, and Azariah, his companions:* **18** *That they would desire mercies of the God of heaven concerning this secret; that Daniel and his fellows should not perish with the rest of the wise men of Babylon.* **19** *Then was the secret revealed unto Daniel in a night vision. Then Daniel blessed the God of heaven.* **20** *Daniel answered and said, Blessed be the name of God for ever and ever: for wisdom and might are his:* **21** *And he changeth the times and the seasons: he removeth kings, and setteth up kings: he giveth wisdom unto the wise, and knowledge to them that know understanding:* **22** *He revealeth the deep and secret things: he knoweth what is in the darkness, and the light dwelleth with him.* **23** *I thank thee, and praise thee, O thou God of my fathers, who hast given me wisdom and might, and hast made known unto me now what we desired of thee: for thou hast now made known unto us the king's matter.* **24** *Therefore Daniel went in unto Arioch, whom the king had ordained to destroy the wise men of Babylon: he went and said* *thus unto him; Destroy not the wise men of Babylon: bring me in before the king, and I will shew unto the king the interpretation. **25** Then Arioch brought in Daniel before the king in haste, and said thus unto him, I have found a man of the captives of Judah, that will make known unto the king the interpretation. **26** The king answered and said to Daniel, whose name was Belteshazzar, Art thou able to make known unto me the dream which I have seen, and the interpretation thereof? **27** Daniel answered in the presence of the king, and said, The secret which the king hath demanded cannot the wise men, the astrologers, the magicians, the soothsayers, shew unto the king; **28** But there is a God in heaven that revealeth secrets, and maketh known to the king Nebuchadnezzar what shall be in the latter days. Thy dream, and the visions of thy head upon thy bed, are these;*

At this point in the text, we will skip ahead past the dream, and then, we will cover the dream itself in the next chapter. Just know for now that Daniel told Nebuchadnezzar what he dreamed and what it meant.

Daniel 2:46 *Then the king Nebuchadnezzar fell upon his face, and worshipped Daniel, and commanded that they should offer an oblation and sweet odours unto him. **47** The king answered unto Daniel, and said, Of a truth it is, that your God is a God of gods, and a Lord of kings, and a revealer of secrets, seeing thou couldest reveal this secret. **48** Then the king made Daniel a great man, and gave him many great gifts, and made him ruler over the whole province of Babylon, and chief of the governors over all the wise men of Babylon. **49** Then Daniel requested of the king, and he set Shadrach, Meshach, and Abednego, over the affairs of the province of Babylon: but Daniel sat in the gate of the king.*

When I was a little kid, like most kids, I often had nightmares. I remember one more than most, because I had it pretty regularly, usually when I was sleeping over at my grandmother's house. In the nightmare I would be playing at the house next door. Suddenly, a hideous floating skull from who knows where would start chasing me. I would run like crazy, but my little legs always did the "won't move right in the dream" thing. I would struggle and struggle and finally make it into grandma's garage. In that garage there is to this day a little room where my grandfather kept his tools. In the dream, I would run into that room and lock the door. I knew the skull was just outside the door, trying to get in. Then, under the door an eerie red light would begin to glow, and I knew that meant that the skull was about to get in... And then I would wake up.

That was a terrifying dream. But the scariest part of all was the night that it changed. That night, when I ran into the little room and locked the door, the red light began to glow, and I woke up just in time, as usual. I was sitting up in bed, panting, glad that I was awake and that the nightmare was over again. But then I noticed that coming up the stairs was a faint, red, eerie glow, getting stronger and **stronger**, and **stronger**... and **then** I woke up, panting, glad that I was awake and the nightmare was over again. But then, I noticed that coming up the stairs was a faint, red, eerie glow, getting stronger and **stronger**, and **stronger**... That happened three times! When I finally did wake up, I did not really believe that I was awake!

A nightmare is bad enough when you are asleep. But when you are pretty sure you are awake, and that the nightmare is real, it is much, much worse.

One of those kind of nightmares happened in Daniel chapter two. Not to Nebuchadnezzar but to everyone else around him! Nebuchadnezzar did have a terrifying nightmare while he was asleep, but it was when he and everyone else woke up that the real nightmare began.

A Forgotten Dream

Daniel 2:1 *And in the second year of the reign of Nebuchadnezzar Nebuchadnezzar dreamed dreams, wherewith his spirit was troubled, and his sleep brake from him.*

When this verse speaks of the second year of Nebuchadnezzar's reign, it is talking about the second year of

36

his reigning alone. He was king along with his father for more than two years before his father's death, so this was the end of the fourth year and beginning of the fifth total year of his reign. That lets us know that Daniel and his three friends had been in captivity for four years at this point. The first three years were the time of testing that we read about in chapter one. So these young men were still brand new to the scene and still very much unknown by the king.

Daniel 2:2 *Then the king commanded to call the magicians, and the astrologers, and the sorcerers, and the Chaldeans, for to shew the king his dreams.* **(Not the meaning just yet, the dream itself. The king was torn up by the dream, but he could not remember what it was!)** *So they came and stood before the king.* **3** *And the king said unto them, I have dreamed a dream, and my spirit was troubled to know the dream.* **4** *Then spake the Chaldeans to the king in Syriack, O king, live for ever: tell thy servants the dream, and we will shew the interpretation.*

There is an interesting little tidbit of information that you might want to know here. The Old Testament was originally written in Hebrew, but not all of it. From this verse which talks about the wise men speaking in Syriak, Daniel is actually written in Syriak until the end of the seventh chapter!

No matter what language they spoke it in, these wise men seemed to know that they were about to be in a bad situation. They are standing before the king, and they actually hear him say, "I've dreamed a dream; I can't remember it; you tell me what it was." Now, these men know good and well that if they make something up, the king is going to know it. A person may not be able to remember a dream, but he will certainly not be fooled into believing he dreamed something that he did not!

So they come back with a counter proposal, "Hey king, tell us the dream that you can't remember, and we'll tell you what it means!"

You see, among people in Bible days, dreams were regarded as having some divine meaning to them. And on

37

occasion, God did speak to men through dreams. We know that now He speaks to men through His Word, the Bible (II Timothy 3:16-17), but in those days He often spoke through dreams.

Because people attached meaning to dreams, the "wise men" of Babylon thought that the king may fall for their proposal. "Just figure out what the dream was, O King, and when you do, we'll tell you what it means, because what it means is obviously far more important than what it was!" Unfortunately for them, the king was no pushover.

5a *The king answered and said to the Chaldeans, The thing is gone from me...*

This dream was terrifying and forgotten! The fear was still there, and the king could not get rid of it because he could not remember it. He just remembered how badly it shook him up. Why was it like this? Because God intended to raise Daniel up to a position of prominence, and in order to do that, Daniel had to come through in the worst of times for the king when everyone else failed. That would set him apart. There is a lesson to be learned here: it is not how we respond in the easy times that set us apart as something special. Anyone can shine during the easy times. It is during the hard times that we can stand out for Jesus.

A Frightening Demand

Daniel 2:5 *The king answered and said to the Chaldeans, The thing is gone from me: if ye will not make known unto me the dream, with the interpretation thereof, ye shall be cut in pieces, and your houses shall be made a dunghill.* **6** *But if ye shew the dream, and the interpretation thereof, ye shall receive of me gifts and rewards and great honour: therefore shew me the dream, and the interpretation thereof.*

When the king said, *Ye shall be cut in pieces, and your houses shall be made a dunghill,* he was speaking literally not figuratively. That is very extreme, very severe, but his power and authority were such that no one could stop him.

38

Nebuchadnezzar was the most authoritative form of earthly king there has ever been. He literally had no limitations to his power, and these men knew it. They were not even thinking of the gifts and rewards and honor he spoke of, because they knew good and well that they could not do what he was asking. So they tried once more to reason with him:

Daniel 2:7 *They answered again and said, Let the king tell his servants the dream, and we will shew the interpretation of it. 8 The king answered and said, I know of certainty that ye would gain the time, because ye see the thing is gone from me. 9 But if ye will not make known unto me the dream, there is but one decree for you: for ye have prepared lying and corrupt words to speak before me, till the time be changed: therefore tell me the dream, and I shall know that ye can shew me the interpretation thereof.*

Nebuchadnezzar, for all of his faults, was no dummy. He knew that these advisors were more wise guys than wise men. If he had told them the dream, they could have and would have given him some "interpretation" of it. And they could do that without him ever knowing if they were wrong. But if they tried to tell him the dream, and it did not hit just right and make him go, "That's it! I remember now!" then he would know they were wrong.

Nebuchadnezzar knew this, and they knew that he knew it. They were stalling for time.

These men had enjoyed a cushy position in Babylon up until this time. But what a difference one night can make. They were all home in bed sleeping in comfort when suddenly they were rousted out of sleep, immediately summoned before the king, and then found out that they only had a few minutes to live if they could not tell the king what he had dreamed and what it meant.

Life is very uncertain. When it gets right down to it, you have no clue when you are going to die or be killed. You might not make it out of this day alive! If you are lost, don't you think you ought to accept Christ as your Savior while you still can?

39

General William Nelson, a Union general in the Civil War, was consumed with the battles in Kentucky when a brawl ended up in his being shot mortally in the chest. He had faced many battles, but the fatal blow came while he was relaxing with his men. As such, he was caught fully unprepared. As men ran up the stairs to help him, the general had just one phrase, "Send for a clergyman; I wish to be baptized." He never had time as an adolescent or young man. He never had time as a private or after he became a general. And his wound did not stop or slow down the war. Everything around him was left virtually unchanged – except for the general's priorities. With only minutes left before he entered eternity, the one thing he cared about was preparing for eternity. He wanted to be baptized. Thirty minutes later he was dead.

Death can come at any moment; every human needs to be ready.

A Furious Decision

Daniel 2:10 *The Chaldeans answered before the king, and said, There is not a man upon the earth that can shew the king's matter:*

There is not a man on earth that can do it? My, my, my, how embarrassed these men were about to be!

...therefore there is no king, lord, nor ruler, that asked such things at any magician, or astrologer, or Chaldean.

Here is where the wise men told the king that he was wrong. That is one of the dumbest things any "wise man" ever did!

Daniel 2:11 *And it is a rare thing that the king requireth, and there is none other that can shew it before the king, except the gods, whose dwelling is not with flesh.*

There is a very interesting fact to take note of at this point. The Chaldeans believed in two types of gods. There were the supreme gods and the inferior gods. The inferior gods had interaction with men, but they were not god enough to solve the problems of men, like say, reminding a man of a dream and telling him what it meant. The superior gods,

40

though, could do those things. In fact, it would be very easy for them to do so. The only problem was, the supreme gods never had any interaction with men. Men were too insignificant for them to bother with. That is what these men meant when they said that these gods *dwelling is not with flesh.*

In other words, "Hey, Nebuchadnezzar, I know you're all furious with us, but it isn't our fault. Blame it on the gods, O King. You're just too insignificant for them to care about, so we can't help you with this!" I wonder how a megalomaniac like Nebuchadnezzar is going to react to that?

Daniel 2:12 *For this cause the king was angry and very furious, and commanded to destroy all the wise men of Babylon.*

Talk about a furious decision! And this all started with a bad dream! May I make an observation here? People are often very prone to overreact. Please do not overreact, over anything, it never helps. Unfortunately for these wise men, Nebuchadnezzar did not have anyone telling him not to overreact.

Daniel 2:13 *And the decree went forth that the wise men should be slain; and they sought Daniel and his fellows to be slain.*

Now pay attention to this. Daniel and his friends were going to be killed along with everyone else, and they did not even know that anything was going on! Please do not whine about how hard you have it until you talk to these four good men and ask them what that was like!

A Faith Displayed

Daniel 2:14 *Then Daniel answered with counsel and wisdom to Arioch the captain of the king's guard, which was gone forth to slay the wise men of Babylon:*

If you want to pattern your life after anyone, consider Daniel. He has just been awakened from sleep by a knock at the door...he opens it up and the executioner is standing there...and he speaks wise, well counseled words to the executioner. On the spur of the moment he demonstrates enough wisdom to save his life and the lives of his three friends, at least for the moment. We should seek hard after wisdom every day and in every situation:

Proverbs 2:10 *When wisdom entereth into thine heart, and knowledge is pleasant unto thy soul;* **11** *Discretion shall preserve thee, understanding shall keep thee:*

Proverbs 3:13 *Happy is the man that findeth wisdom, and the man that getteth understanding.*

Proverbs 4:7 *Wisdom is the principal thing; therefore get wisdom: and with all thy getting get understanding.*

Proverbs 8:11 *For wisdom is better than rubies; and all the things that may be desired are not to be compared to it.*

Seek after and pray for wisdom. Daniel did, and it saved his life!

Daniel 2:15 *He answered and said to Arioch the king's captain, Why is the decree so hasty from the king? Then Arioch made the thing known to Daniel.*

That was an excellent question, the product of wisdom. Daniel wanted to know what could make the king get into such a hurry to see some very good assets die. So Arioch told him everything that had happened. Again, how Biblical:

Proverbs 18:13 *He that answereth a matter before he heareth it, it is folly and shame unto him.*

Daniel did not jump to conclusions; he got the facts. Then he acted on them:

Daniel 2:16 *Then Daniel went in, and desired of the king that he would give him time, and that he would shew the king the interpretation.*

I love this. Daniel, to save his life, might have been tempted to go in and ask the king to tell him the dream, so that he could interpret it. But you see, by asking questions, he had already found out that the other guys had tried that and it did not work. This is called "learning from the mistakes of others," which is always a better idea than having to learn from your own mistakes.

Daniel did not do what the other men had tried. As a very young man, he marched in before the king (the most powerful man on earth), stood there, and calmly informed the king that if he would give him a little time he would do exactly what the king was asking. That is displaying some faith!

Daniel 2:17 *Then Daniel went to his house, and made the thing known to Hananiah, Mishael, and Azariah, his companions:* **18** *That they would desire mercies of the God of heaven concerning this secret; that Daniel and his fellows should not perish with the rest of the wise men of Babylon.*

Daniel is getting wiser and wiser by the minute. Rather than wracking his brain and pacing the floor, the first thing he does is get some people praying! Look at the result:

Daniel 2:19a *Then was the secret revealed unto Daniel in a night vision.*

Think quickly. You are Daniel. Your life is on the line, and the king is in a hurry. You have just gotten the information you need to save your life. What do you do next if it is you? You very likely run straight to the king! But look what Daniel did:

Daniel 2:19b *Then Daniel blessed the God of heaven.* **20** *Daniel answered and said, Blessed be the name of God for ever and ever: for wisdom and might are his:*

There is always time for us to be grateful. If we are in too big of a hurry to say "thank you" to God or man, we may as well go ahead and die, because we are way too busy to live.

Daniel 2:21 *And he changeth the times and the seasons: he removeth kings, and setteth up kings: he giveth wisdom unto the wise, and knowledge to them that know understanding:* **22** *He revealeth the deep and secret things: he knoweth what is in the darkness, and the light dwelleth with him.*

Daniel said what he said in those last two verses because of what was in the dream. We will cover that in the next chapter, and I will remind you of Daniel's words here.

Daniel 2:23 *I thank thee, and praise thee, O thou God of my fathers, who hast given me wisdom and might, and hast made known unto me now what we desired of thee: for thou hast now made known unto us the king's matter.* **24** *Therefore*

43

Daniel went in unto Arioch, whom the king had ordained to destroy the wise men of Babylon: he went and said thus unto him; Destroy not the wise men of Babylon: bring me in before the king, and I will shew unto the king the interpretation. **25** *Then Arioch brought in Daniel before the king in haste, and said thus unto him, I have found a man of the captives of Judah, that will make known unto the king the interpretation.*

By the way, this is hilarious. Arioch, the guy who was going to kill Daniel, is now taking credit for finding him!

Daniel 2:26 *The king answered and said to Daniel, whose name was Belteshazzar, Art thou able to make known unto me the dream which I have seen, and the interpretation thereof?* **27** *Daniel answered in the presence of the king, and said, The secret which the king hath demanded cannot the wise men, the astrologers, the magicians, the soothsayers, shew unto the king;* **28** *But there is a God in heaven that revealeth secrets, and maketh known to the king Nebuchadnezzar what shall be in the latter days. Thy dream, and the visions of thy head upon thy bed, are these;*

Pay attention to what Daniel did. Daniel, by what he said, did not just contradict what the wise men had said about the matter being impossible; he also let Nebuchadnezzar know that his Babylonian view of God was wrong. The real God, the supreme God, not only has the power to help man, He is willing and able to help man. The God we serve is ever present, and our ever present help in time of trouble.

A Fruitful Development

Daniel 2:46 *Then the king Nebuchadnezzar fell upon his face, and worshipped Daniel, and commanded that they should offer an oblation and sweet odours unto him.* **47** *The king answered unto Daniel, and said, Of a truth it is, that your God is a God of gods, and a Lord of kings, and a revealer of secrets, seeing thou couldest reveal this secret.*

Because of Daniel's faith, Nebuchadnezzar is now beginning to be aware of God. He is not saved yet, but the process has begun.

44

Daniel 2:48 *Then the king made Daniel a great man, and gave him many great gifts, and made him ruler over the whole province of Babylon, and chief of the governors over all the wise men of Babylon.*

Remember those home-grown Babylonian guys who told the king that no one could do it? The king just made Daniel, the foreigner, their boss. Remember that, it will come into play later on in the book.

Daniel 2:49 *Then Daniel requested of the king, and he set Shadrach, Meshach, and Abednego, over the affairs of the province of Babylon: but Daniel sat in the gate of the king.*

This is one more thing to respect about Daniel. He did not forget his friends on the way up. So many do, but Daniel did not.

*   *   *   *   *

The worst kind of nightmare is the real live wide awake kind. How will you deal with them? Make sure you are saved, use wisdom, get praying, demonstrate faith, give God the glory, and when things turn out well, do not forget the friends that helped you through it.

Chapter 4

Unmasking the Monster

Daniel 2:28 *But there is a God in heaven that revealeth secrets, and maketh known to the king Nebuchadnezzar what shall be in the latter days. Thy dream, and the visions of thy head upon thy bed, are these;* **29** *As for thee, O king, thy thoughts came into thy mind upon thy bed, what should come to pass hereafter: and he that revealeth secrets maketh known to thee what shall come to pass.* **30** *But as for me, this secret is not revealed to me for any wisdom that I have more than any living, but for their sakes that shall make known the interpretation to the king, and that thou mightest know the thoughts of thy heart.* **31** *Thou, O king, sawest, and behold a great image. This great image, whose brightness was excellent, stood before thee; and the form thereof was terrible.* **32** *This image's head was of fine gold, his breast and his arms of silver, his belly and his thighs of brass,* **33** *His legs of iron, his feet part of iron and part of clay.* **34** *Thou sawest till that a stone was cut out without hands, which smote the image upon his feet that were of iron and clay, and brake them to pieces.* **35** *Then was the iron, the clay, the brass, the silver, and the gold, broken to pieces together, and became like the chaff of the summer threshingfloors; and the wind carried them away, that no place was found for them: and the stone that smote the image became a great mountain, and filled the whole earth.* **36**

This is the dream; and we will tell the interpretation thereof before the king. **37** *Thou, O king, art a king of kings: for the God of heaven hath given thee a kingdom, power, and strength, and glory.* **38** *And wheresoever the children of men dwell, the beasts of the field and the fowls of the heaven hath he given into thine hand, and hath made thee ruler over them all. Thou art this head of gold.* **39** *And after thee shall arise another kingdom inferior to thee, and another third kingdom of brass, which shall bear rule over all the earth.* **40** *And the fourth kingdom shall be strong as iron: forasmuch as iron breaketh in pieces and subdueth all things: and as iron that breaketh all these, shall it break in pieces and bruise.* **41** *And whereas thou sawest the feet and toes, part of potters' clay, and part of iron, the kingdom shall be divided; but there shall be in it of the strength of the iron, forasmuch as thou sawest the iron mixed with miry clay.* **42** *And as the toes of the feet were part of iron, and part of clay, so the kingdom shall be partly strong, and partly broken.* **43** *And whereas thou sawest iron mixed with miry clay, they shall mingle themselves with the seed of men: but they shall not cleave one to another, even as iron is not mixed with clay.* **44** *And in the days of these kings shall the God of heaven set up a kingdom, which shall never be destroyed: and the kingdom shall not be left to other people, but it shall break in pieces and consume all these kingdoms, and it shall stand for ever.* **45** *Forasmuch as thou sawest that the stone was cut out of the mountain without hands, and that it brake in pieces the iron, the brass, the clay, the silver, and the gold; the great God hath made known to the king what shall come to pass hereafter: and the dream is certain, and the interpretation thereof sure.*

To properly set the stage for this chapter, let me briefly remind you of what happened in the last chapter, which covered the verses before and after our text for this section. King Nebuchadnezzar had a dream. It was awful, terrifying, and was all the worse because even though he knew it was awful and terrifying, he could not remember what it was. He forgot the dream!

When most people forget a dream, that is just too bad for them. But when you are Nebuchadnezzar, the most powerful human king that has ever lived, nothing is ever "too bad for you." Nebuchadnezzar called in his Chaldean wise men and made a simple little demand of them. "Tell me what my forgotten dream was and tell me what it means. Oh, and by the way, if you don't, I'll cut you into pieces and make your houses into dung hills."

The Chaldeans knew they couldn't do it. So they basically told Nebuchadnezzar that it wasn't their fault; the god's just did not think that Nebuchadnezzar was important enough to bother with. A split second later, the order went out to kill all the wise men in Babylon. The problem with that was that Daniel, Shadrach, Meshach, and Abednego were considered wise men. They were about to die, and they did not even know anything was going on!

Daniel, using wisdom far beyond his years, went in before the king and told him that if he would give him a little time, he would tell him the dream and the meaning. Then he went home, got his three friends praying, and soon, God gave him the answer.

In the last chapter we skipped ahead to what happened when Daniel went in and told Nebuchadnezzar the dream and the meaning. In this chapter we are going to cover what we skipped last time, the dream itself. We are going to unmask the monster.

The Introduction to the Dream

Daniel 2:28 *But there is a God in heaven that revealeth secrets, and maketh known to the king Nebuchadnezzar* **what shall be in the latter days**. *Thy dream, and the visions of thy head upon thy bed, are these;* **29** *As for thee, O king, thy thoughts came into thy mind upon thy bed, what should come to pass hereafter: and he that revealeth secrets maketh known to thee what shall come to pass.* **30** *But as for me, this secret is not revealed to me for any wisdom that I have more than any living, but for their sakes that shall make known the* *interpretation to the king, and that thou mightest know the thoughts of thy heart.*

There are two things to notice here. First of all, this dream was not made known just because of Daniel's wisdom; it was also made known for Daniel's sake... as well as for Shadrach, Meshach, and Abednego. God cared about those four. It was also made known so that Nebuchadnezzar could know the thoughts of his heart. In other words, it was important to God that Nebuchadnezzar know the details of the dream, because God expected the king to live within the confines that God set forth in the dream. Remember that, it will be very important in the next chapter.

The second thing to notice is that three different times in the verses we just read, Daniel told Nebuchadnezzar that this dream was a prophecy. It was about the latter days, the hereafter, the things which would come to pass.

There are a great many dreams in the Bible. But understand this: when it comes to understanding God's plan for nations and kingdoms through the ages, this is the most important dream in the entire Bible. Let me say this as well: when it comes to dreams that verify that the Bible is the Word of God, this is one of the most important dreams in the Bible. I will show you why I say that in just a little while.

The Identity of the Dream

What exactly was this dream? Here it is:

Daniel 2:31 *Thou, O king, sawest, and behold a great image. This great image, whose brightness was excellent, stood before thee; and the form thereof was terrible.* **32** *This image's head was of fine gold, his breast and his arms of silver, his belly and his thighs of brass,* **33** *His legs of iron, his feet part of iron and part of clay.* **34** *Thou sawest till that a stone was cut out without hands, which smote the image upon his feet that were of iron and clay, and brake them to pieces.* **35** *Then was the iron, the clay, the brass, the silver, and the gold, broken to pieces together, and became like the chaff of the summer threshingfloors; and the wind carried them away, that* *no place was found for them: and the stone that smote the image became a great mountain, and filled the whole earth.* **36a** *This is the dream...*

The dream that shook Nebuchadnezzar up so badly was absolutely odd. Who do you know that has ever had a dream like this? This is not your typical monster/riding a lawn-mower that ends up flying/giving a speech and realizing you are in your underwear kind of dream.

This was a dream about a statue. A HUGE statue. It was bright and gleaming, and the text says that its form was "terrible." That Hebrew word indicates something that when you looked at it would scare you to death just by its appearance. It was a huge, scary statue in the shape of a man.

This statue was constructed in the oddest of ways. The head of the statue was made of gold. The upper chest and the two arms were made of silver. The stomach and thigh area was made of brass. The legs below the thighs were made of iron. The feet were made partly of iron and partly of clay. All of this came flooding back to Nebuchadnezzar's memory as Daniel spoke of it. He remembered it vividly. He could see the image in his mind, this weird concoction that started off as gold and ended up as iron and clay.

I do not know how long Nebuchadnezzar stared at that image in his dream. But I do know that by the time the dream ended, that statue was gone. In the dream Nebuchadnezzar saw a huge stone not made or shaped by any human hands. That stone came rolling into the picture and smashed into the feet of the statue. The whole statue came crashing down and broke into pieces.

But even the broken pieces did not survive. That stone broke them into nothing more than chaff. That great statue was literally reduced to a worthless pile of dust. But even the dust of the statue did not survive. The wind blew it all away, and there was no place found for a single scrap of the statue's dust; it literally ceased to exist entirely. All that was left to look at was the rock. That rock began to grow, and grow, and grow, until it filled the entire earth. The statue was gone, and only the rock that destroyed it remained.

The Interpretation of the Dream

Daniel 2:36 *This is the dream; and we will tell the interpretation thereof before the king.* **37** *Thou, O king, art a king of kings: for the God of heaven hath given thee a kingdom, power, and strength, and glory.* **38** *And wheresoever the children of men dwell, the beasts of the field and the fowls of the heaven hath he given into thine hand, and hath made thee ruler over them all. Thou art this head of gold.*

Every ounce of power and authority that Nebuchadnezzar had, God had given it to him. Never forget this: God puts even wicked men in authority to accomplish His own purposes. No president, no matter how bad, ever gets elected without God placing that man in the White House. No dictator ever arises without God giving him the power that he then abuses.

You see, God sometimes places good men in authority as blessings when His people do right and bad men in authority as punishment when His people do wrong. Nebuchadnezzar was not a good king, but he was king because God made him king.

God not only made him king, He made him the most powerful human king in all of history. He gave him charge over every man, woman, child, bird, and beast on the planet. Nebuchadnezzar was the head of gold in the image. The king was in this case synonymous with the kingdom. That head represented Nebuchadnezzar and also the Babylonian Empire that he, at that time, was in charge of. That empire would have two more kings after him, but it would always be "Nebuchadnezzar's kingdom"

What part of the image was Nebuchadnezzar? *The head.* Remember that when we get into the next chapter.

Daniel 2:39a *And after thee shall arise another kingdom inferior to thee,*

The first metal used in the statue was gold. Silver is inferior to gold. The kingdom that would follow the Babylonian Kingdom was not going to be as strong as the Babylonian Kingdom had been in its heyday. Now let me ask you this: do you remember what part of the statue was silver? The torso and the two arms. Do you remember who the Babylonians eventually fell to? The Medes and the Persians. Two arms, two kingdoms united together. Neither one would be strong enough to take on Babylon alone, so they banded together to do it.

Please understand this, no one could have seen this coming. When Daniel uttered this prophecy from the dream of Nebuchadnezzar, the Medes and the Persians were no threat at all, and there was no indication that they ever would be. It would be nearly seventy years before this prophecy came to pass.

Nebuchadnezzar had reigned supremely, the head of gold, every word he said was law when he said it. But Daniel said that the next kingdom would be "inferior" to that. The Medes and Persians operated very much by committee. The nobles of the provinces shared power with the king. It took them a lot longer to get things done. There was no one person to call the shots. It was certainly fairer to its people, but it was far less powerful. It was only going to be silver, where Babylon was gold.

Daniel 2:39b *...and another third kingdom of brass, which shall bear rule over all the earth.*

Every part of this dream is described in much greater detail later on in the book of Daniel, which helps us to know exactly who was being spoken of in each part. This third part of the prophecy foretold the coming of the Grecian Empire. Again, this is something that no one saw coming. It would be like a "prophet" today predicting that in 130 or so years, New Hampshire would rule the world!

Even in the few days before it came to pass, no one believed it would or could come to pass. The king of Persia knew that Greece was coming to war against him. But Greece and her armies were tiny compared to the size and strength of Persia. The Jewish historian Josephus tells us that the king of Persia also did not think that the leader of Greece was much of a threat. You may have heard of him; we call him "Alexander the Great." Alexander used speed, maneuvering, and a host of brand-new tactics no one had ever seen in war before to defeat the mighty Persian army.

What metal represented Greece? Brass. Does anyone want to guess what metal the Greek soldiers became famous for wearing? Brass. God knew this before it happened. The Grecian Empire, the empire of brass, defeated the Persian Empire of silver which had defeated the Babylonian Empire of gold. Persia was not as pure and powerful as Babylon had been in her prime, and Greece was not as pure and powerful as Persia had been in her prime.

Daniel 2:40 *And the fourth kingdom shall be strong as iron: forasmuch as iron breaketh in pieces and subdueth all things: and as iron that breaketh all these, shall it break in pieces and bruise.*

The fourth kingdom that Nebuchadnezzar saw was the kingdom of Rome. Again, this could not have ever been predicted. This kingdom, Rome, was not made of a precious or decorative metal like gold, silver, or brass. Rome was sheer power and represented by iron. God described it here as a kingdom that would bruise and break in pieces all of the others. Rome was positively brutal. It was not nearly as pure or precious as the others but far longer lasting. Rome was the empire in power at the time of Christ, during the time of the apostles, and for hundreds of years thereafter. But here is where things get truly interesting:

Daniel 2:41 *And whereas thou sawest the feet and toes, part of potters' clay, and part of iron, the kingdom shall be divided; but there shall be in it of the strength of the iron, forasmuch as thou sawest the iron mixed with miry clay.*

When we look at what happened to the Babylonian Empire and realize that there is no real trace of it on earth anymore, doesn't the word "destroyed" describe it accurately?

54

Yes. When we look at what happened to the Persian Empire and realize that there is very little left of it on earth anymore, doesn't the word "destroyed" describe it accurately? Yes. When we look at what happened to the Grecian Empire and realize that there is no real trace of it on earth anymore, even though there is a tiny country that still bears its name, doesn't the word "destroyed" describe it accurately? Yes.

But when it comes to the Roman Empire, please notice that God did not picure them as being "destroyed." In verse forty-one He used the word "divided." The Roman Empire has never ceased to exist for even a day. She fell into disrepair, divided into parts, and became some things you may have heard of: France, Spain, Germany, Great Britain, Italy, all of Europe!   And of all of the kingdoms represented by Nebuchadnezzar's dream, Rome is the only one that has a "round two" as a world super power. Look at this:

Daniel 2:42 *And as the toes of the feet were part of iron, and part of clay, so the kingdom shall be partly strong, and partly broken.* **43** *And whereas thou sawest iron mixed with miry clay, they shall mingle themselves with the seed of men: but they shall not cleave one to another, even as iron is not mixed with clay.*

When you read the rest of the book of Daniel and the book of the Revelation, you find that the Antichrist is going to lead a ten-part federation, a revival of the Roman Empire. But as you look at these verses, you see that whereas the first Rome was all iron, that which is to come will be part iron and part clay.   There will be a mixture of the Roman and the non-Roman, there will be some nations in the federation that are weak, some that are strong. When that comes to pass, which will have its final form during the Tribulation Period, the last part of Nebuchadnezzar's dream will happen:

Daniel 2:44 *And in the days of these kings shall the God of heaven set up a kingdom, which shall never be destroyed: and the kingdom shall not be left to other people, but it shall break in pieces and consume all these kingdoms, and it shall stand for ever.* **45** *Forasmuch as thou sawest that* *the stone was cut out of the mountain without hands, and that it brake in pieces the iron, the brass, the clay, the silver, and the gold; the great God hath made known to the king what shall come to pass hereafter: and the dream is certain, and the interpretation thereof sure.*

That rock is none other than the Lord Jesus Christ and His coming kingdom. He is the Rock which was not cut or formed by man. When He comes, the last great gentile world kingdom will be in power. Nebuchadnezzar will have come and gone, Darius and Cyrus will have come and gone, Alexander will have come and gone, the Caesars will have come and gone, and the Antichrist will be in charge. Jesus will come barreling down from Heaven like a runaway boulder and crush the last remaining vestiges of Nebuchadnezzar's image.

This verse says that the dream is *certain* and the interpretation *sure*. In other words, this is the way it is going to happen, and no one can stop it.

As we begin to draw this chapter to a close, let me make a few important applications from what we have learned:

1.   We can know that the Bible is God's Word because of such detailed fulfilled prophecy.

2.   All of these kingdoms lined themselves up against God's people, Israel, and all of them fell because of it. If America ever assaults Israel, she will fall as well. We must continue to demand that our leaders support God's chosen people!

3.   That Rock is getting ready to roll. We are already seeing nations in the region of Rome unify, and the world is already rumbling about a "real leader," a man who can unite us all. That man will be the Antichrist, and you can bet that if he showed up today, the world would flock

after him.   If you are not saved, you will be crushed by that Rock.

Luke 20:17 *And he beheld them, and said, What is this then that is written, The stone which the builders rejected, the same is become the head of the corner?* **18** *Whosoever shall fall upon that stone shall be broken; but on whomsoever it shall fall, it will grind him to powder.*

That was Christ speaking of Himself. One of the most awful ways to die is to be crushed. You have seen the prophecy, you know this is the Word of God, you know you need to be saved. All of the warning flags are out, people are waving their arms and shouting for you to move, the Rock is tumbling down, if you get crushed by Christ instead of converted by Christ you have no one to blame but yourself.

Chapter 5
1, 2, 3, 4

Daniel 3:1 *Nebuchadnezzar the king made an image of gold, whose height was threescore cubits, and the breadth thereof six cubits: he set it up in the plain of Dura, in the province of Babylon.* **2** *Then Nebuchadnezzar the king sent to gather together the princes, the governors, and the captains, the judges, the treasurers, the counsellors, the sheriffs, and all the rulers of the provinces, to come to the dedication of the image which Nebuchadnezzar the king had set up.* **3** *Then the princes, the governors, and captains, the judges, the treasurers, the counsellors, the sheriffs, and all the rulers of the provinces, were gathered together unto the dedication of the image that Nebuchadnezzar the king had set up; and they stood before the image that Nebuchadnezzar had set up.* **4** *Then an herald cried aloud, To you it is commanded, O people, nations, and languages,* **5** *That at what time ye hear the sound of the cornet, flute, harp, sackbut, psaltery, dulcimer, and all kinds of musick, ye fall down and worship the golden image that Nebuchadnezzar the king hath set up:* **6** *And whoso falleth not down and worshippeth shall the same hour be cast into the midst of a burning fiery furnace.* **7** *Therefore at that time, when all the people heard the sound of the cornet, flute, harp, sackbut, psaltery, and all kinds of musick, all the people, the nations, and the languages, fell down and worshipped the* *golden image that Nebuchadnezzar the king had set up.* **8** *Wherefore at that time certain Chaldeans came near, and accused the Jews.* **9** *They spake and said to the king Nebuchadnezzar, O king, live for ever.* **10** *Thou, O king, hast made a decree, that every man that shall hear the sound of the cornet, flute, harp, sackbut, psaltery, and dulcimer, and all kinds of musick, shall fall down and worship the golden image:* **11** *And whoso falleth not down and worshippeth, that he should be cast into the midst of a burning fiery furnace.* **12** *There are certain Jews whom thou hast set over the affairs of the province of Babylon, Shadrach, Meshach, and Abednego; these men, O king, have not regarded thee: they serve not thy gods, nor worship the golden image which thou hast set up.* **13** *Then Nebuchadnezzar in his rage and fury commanded to bring Shadrach, Meshach, and Abednego. Then they brought these men before the king.* **14** *Nebuchadnezzar spake and said unto them, Is it true, O Shadrach, Meshach, and Abednego, do not ye serve my gods, nor worship the golden image which I have set up?* **15** *Now if ye be ready that at what time ye hear the sound of the cornet, flute, harp, sackbut, psaltery, and dulcimer, and all kinds of musick, ye fall down and worship the image which I have made; well: but if ye worship not, ye shall be cast the same hour into the midst of a burning fiery furnace; and who is that God that shall deliver you out of my hands?* **16** *Shadrach, Meshach, and Abednego, answered and said to the king, O Nebuchadnezzar, we are not careful to answer thee in this matter.* **17** *If it be so, our God whom we serve is able to deliver us from the burning fiery furnace, and he will deliver us out of thine hand, O king.* **18** *But if not, be it known unto thee, O king, that we will not serve thy gods, nor worship the golden image which thou hast set up.* **19** *Then was Nebuchadnezzar full of fury, and the form of his visage was changed against Shadrach, Meshach, and Abednego: therefore he spake, and commanded that they should heat the furnace one seven times more than it was wont to be heated.* **20** *And he commanded the most mighty men that were in his army to bind Shadrach, Meshach, and Abednego, and to cast them into the* *burning fiery furnace.* **21** *Then these men were bound in their coats, their hosen, and their hats, and their other garments, and were cast into the midst of the burning fiery furnace.* **22** *Therefore because the king's commandment was urgent, and the furnace exceeding hot, the flame of the fire slew those men that took up Shadrach, Meshach, and Abednego.* **23** *And these three men, Shadrach, Meshach, and Abednego, fell down bound into the midst of the burning fiery furnace.* **24** *Then Nebuchadnezzar the king was astonied, and rose up in haste, and spake, and said unto his counsellors, Did not we cast three men bound into the midst of the fire? They answered and said unto the king, True, O king.* **25** *He answered and said, Lo, I see four men loose, walking in the midst of the fire, and they have no hurt; and the form of the fourth is like the Son of God.* **26** *Then Nebuchadnezzar came near to the mouth of the burning fiery furnace, and spake, and said, Shadrach, Meshach, and Abednego, ye servants of the most high God, come forth, and come hither. Then Shadrach, Meshach, and Abednego, came forth of the midst of the fire.* **27** *And the princes, governors, and captains, and the king's counsellors, being gathered together, saw these men, upon whose bodies the fire had no power, nor was an hair of their head singed, neither were their coats changed, nor the smell of fire had passed on them.* **28** *Then Nebuchadnezzar spake, and said, Blessed be the God of Shadrach, Meshach, and Abednego, who hath sent his angel, and delivered his servants that trusted in him, and have changed the king's word, and yielded their bodies, that they might not serve nor worship any god, except their own God.* **29** *Therefore I make a decree, That every people, nation, and language, which speak any thing amiss against the God of Shadrach, Meshach, and Abednego, shall be cut in pieces, and their houses shall be made a dunghill: because there is no other God that can deliver after this sort.* **30** *Then the king promoted Shadrach, Meshach, and Abednego, in the province of Babylon.*

We have focused much on Daniel thus far. This chapter will not mention him, as the focus turns to his three friends,

Shadrach, Meshach, and Abednego. This chapter is all about the numbers, which start off looking not so good at all.

1 Metal Used in the Image

Daniel 3:1 *Nebuchadnezzar the king made an image of gold, whose height was threescore cubits, and the breadth thereof six cubits: he set it up in the plain of Dura, in the province of Babylon.*

In the last chapter, you surely remember that Nebuchadnezzar had a dream. That dream was about a huge image made of multiple metals. The head was made of gold and represented Nebuchadnezzar and the kingdom of Babylon. The torso and two arms were made of silver and represented the Medo-Persian Empire. The thighs and belly were of brass and represented the Grecian Empire. The lower legs were of iron and represented the Roman Empire. The feet and toes were a mixture of iron and clay and represented the revived Roman Empire, which will be formed during the Tribulation Period under the rule of the Antichrist. One statue, four metals, four kingdoms. That was the plan of God for the ages. It was His schedule for Gentile world powers.

But Nebuchadnezzar had what he believed was a better plan. How many metals did God have in the image? *Four.* But when Nebuchadnezzar built his image, how many metals did he use? *One.* And not surprisingly, it was not silver or brass or iron, but gold that he used. He built an image which was 90 feet high and 9 feet wide and made all of gold. One – one metal used in the image.

Let me just stop and make a few applications here:

First, be happy with what God gives you.

God gave Nebuchadnezzar the choicest part of the statue, but he was not happy with that; it was not enough for him. People need to learn to be happy with what God gives them and quit wanting what God has given them plus what God has given others. That would eliminate affairs and robbery and blackmail and a host of other wicked things.

Second, be prepared for eternity, because you are not going to live forever.

Nebuchadnezzar was only the head of the statue. He was not going to live forever. But he had been told, "O King, live forever," so many times, he actually started to believe it. Be prepared for eternity because you are not going to live forever. Nebuchadnezzar did not, and you will not!

Third, build people, because the things you build will not last forever.

The head represented the king, but it also represented his kingdom, Babylon. Babylon was the greatest kingdom ever, but it had an expiration date. Nebuchadnezzar spent so much time building it up and making it great, but very little time building up people.

One – one metal used in the image.

2 Simple Commands: Fall Down and Worship

Daniel 3:2 *Then Nebuchadnezzar the king sent to gather together the princes, the governors, and the captains, the judges, the treasurers, the counsellors, the sheriffs, and all the rulers of the provinces, to come to the dedication of the image which Nebuchadnezzar the king had set up.* **3** *Then the princes, the governors, and captains, the judges, the treasurers, the counsellors, the sheriffs, and all the rulers of the provinces, were gathered together unto the dedication of the image that Nebuchadnezzar the king had set up; and they stood before the image that Nebuchadnezzar had set up.*

Everyone who was anyone was gathered together for this "monumental occasion." Every eye was focused, jaws were gaping open.

Daniel 3:4 *Then an herald cried aloud, To you it is commanded, O people, nations, and languages,* **5** *That at what time ye hear the sound of the cornet, flute, harp, sackbut, psaltery, dulcimer, and all kinds of musick, ye fall down and worship the golden image that Nebuchadnezzar the king hath set up:*

Nebuchadnezzar made a god for the people. The god was basically a statue of himself. He commanded that when the music began to play (and by the way, isn't it interesting that even way back then, music was used to get people to do wrong!) everyone must fall down on their faces and worship that image. Then he gave a little "incentive" to make sure that everyone would obey:

Daniel 3:6 *And whoso falleth not down and worshippeth shall the same hour be cast into the midst of a burning fiery furnace.*

By the way, everyone knew that this may have been an "idol" threat, but it certainly was no "idle" threat. Statues like this were made from a smelting furnace, which would have been right there on hand. Nebuchandnezzar had the tools available to make good on his threat.

How did this go for Nebuchadnezzar?

Daniel 3:7 *Therefore at that time, when all the people heard the sound of the cornet, flute, harp, sackbut, psaltery, and all kinds of musick, all the people, the nations, and the languages, fell down and worshipped the golden image that Nebuchadnezzar the king had set up.*

Apparently it went pretty well!

One – one metal used in the image. Two – two simple commands.

3 Boys Who Stood When Everyone Else Bowed

Daniel 3:8 *Wherefore at that time certain Chaldeans came near, and accused the Jews.* **9** *They spake and said to the king Nebuchadnezzar, O king, live for ever.* **10** *Thou, O king, hast made a decree, that every man that shall hear the sound of the cornet, flute, harp, sackbut, psaltery, and dulcimer, and all kinds of musick, shall fall down and worship the golden image:* **11** *And whoso falleth not down and worshippeth, that he should be cast into the midst of a burning fiery furnace.* **12** *There are certain Jews whom thou hast set over the affairs of the province of Babylon, Shadrach, Meshach, and Abednego;*

these men, O king, have not regarded thee: they serve not thy gods, nor worship the golden image which thou hast set up.

This accusation was true; these three boys would not bow. By the way, the obvious question here is "where was Daniel?" The answer is – we have no idea, but we do know that he was not there, or he would not have been bowing either.

Daniel 3:13 *Then Nebuchadnezzar in his rage and fury commanded to bring Shadrach, Meshach, and Abednego. Then they brought these men before the king.* **14** *Nebuchadnezzar spake and said unto them, Is it true, O Shadrach, Meshach, and Abednego, do not ye serve my gods, nor worship the golden image which I have set up?* **15** *Now if ye be ready that at what time ye hear the sound of the cornet, flute, harp, sackbut, psaltery, and dulcimer, and all kinds of musick, ye fall down and worship the image which I have made; well: but if ye worship not, ye shall be cast the same hour into the midst of a burning fiery furnace; and who is that God that shall deliver you out of my hands?*

I love that last question from Nebuchadnezzar. "Who is that God? Who do you think you're serving? You better reconsider your choices, boys, because my name is Nebuchadnezzar, and if you don't bow down on verse two, I'm going to throw you into the burning fiery furnace. And who is that God that shall deliver you out of my hands?"

Do you understand the arrogance of that question? If Nebuchadnezzar had claimed to be the most powerful man on earth, he would have been correct. But Nebuchadnezzar was claiming to be more powerful than any god anywhere anytime. He was claiming to be more powerful than any of his own false gods, and he was most assuredly claiming to be more powerful than the God of the Hebrews, Jehovah God.

Well, Nebuchadnezzar asked a question, so it was up to those three boys to provide him with an answer:

Daniel 3:16 *Shadrach, Meshach, and Abednego, answered and said to the king, O Nebuchadnezzar, we are not careful to answer thee in this matter* **(we aren't trembling in fear, and we don't have to think this through and choose**

65

our words very carefully. We aren't "walking on eggshells" as we answer). *17 If it be so, our God whom we serve is able to deliver us from the burning fiery furnace, and he will deliver us out of thine hand, O king.* **18** *But if not, be it known unto thee, O king, that we will not serve thy gods, nor worship the golden image which thou hast set up.*

The answer that these three boys gave is among the most profound anywhere in the Bible. It tells a lot about God and a lot about how we are to react and respond to God. Look at a few things:

One, they knew God was able to deliver them, even though it seemed impossible.

Two, they also knew that God might not choose to deliver them, even though He could! In every trial, we are convinced that the greatest thing that could happen is for God to deliver us. But it may be that God has an even greater thing in mind by not delivering us. God may choose to deliver us or those we love from life-threatening sicknesses. That would be wonderful. But He could choose to let us experience the greatest of sorrows and by that draw us nearer to Himself than we could have ever imagined.

God may choose to deliver us financially. Or not. Either way is great. If He does, we shout the victory and testify of His goodness. But maybe if He does not, we learn in the future how to avoid the mistakes that we made in the past. These boys knew that God could deliver them, but they also knew that He might have a very good reason not to.

Three, they were determined to do right even if God did not deliver them. Look at it again:

Daniel 3:18 *But if not, be it known unto thee, O king, that we will not serve thy gods, nor worship the golden image which thou hast set up.*

"Nebuchadnezzar, God could deliver us, but He may not choose to. But that is really irrelevant to us. The fact is, we are not going to serve your false gods no matter what."

That statement by these boys is often chalked up to faith. "Man, those guys had a lot of faith in God!" I am sure

66

they did. But listen to me, this really had very little to do with faith. It had everything to do with love! They really had no clue whether or not God was going to deliver them. But they did not care whether God did or did not deliver them. They just knew that they loved Him, they were devoted to Him, and they were not going to do anything to disappoint Him.

Let me tell you what the difference is between kids in church youth groups. First of all, many kids that think they are saved are really lost, and that explains why they can not seem to do right. But even among the ones that are truly saved, you will find some that always seem to do right and have a good spirit, and some that are at times as carnal, immodest, and as worldly as they come. Here is the difference: some of them love God and some of them do not. If a person loves God, they will do right even when no one from the church or family is watching. If a person loves God, they will not put immodest pictures online. If a person loves God, they will not give away their virginity before marriage. If a person loves God, they will not date unsaved people because they know God's Word forbids it.

In any issue of sin, loving God will make the difference. It is time for people who are truly saved to be like these three Hebrew boys and really love God. I wonder, do you truly love God right now more than anything or anyone?

One – one metal used in the image. Two – two simple commands, bow down and worship. Three – three boys who would not bow...

4 Men in the Fire

Daniel 3:19 *Then was Nebuchadnezzar full of fury, and the form of his visage was changed against Shadrach, Meshach, and Abednego: therefore he spake, and commanded that they should heat the furnace one seven times more than it was wont to be heated.* **20** *And he commanded the most mighty men that were in his army to bind Shadrach, Meshach, and Abednego, and to cast them into the burning fiery furnace.* **21** *Then these men were bound in their coats, their hosen, and*

67

their hats, and their other garments, and were cast into the midst of the burning fiery furnace. **22** *Therefore because the king's commandment was urgent, and the furnace exceeding hot, the flame of the fire slew those men that took up Shadrach, Meshach, and Abednego.* **23** *And these three men, Shadrach, Meshach, and Abednego, fell down bound into the midst of the burning fiery furnace.*

Nebuchadnezzar had never been this angry. Three boys with no power at all were defying his command, and even worse, showed no fear before him. So the king had the furnace heated up to far beyond what OSHA would allow today, seven times above normal temperature. Normal temperature would melt metal, and this was seven times worse!

Shadrach, Meshach, and Abednego were all decked out in their finest. They were bound fully clothed, and the mightiest soldiers Nebuchadnezzar had threw them into the furnace. The furnace was so hot that those soldiers died throwing the boys in. Nebuchadnezzar was seated on a perch high above it all and was able to view what was happening down in the flames.

Daniel 3:24 *Then Nebuchadnezzar the king was astonied, and rose up in haste, and spake, and said unto his counsellors, Did not we cast three men bound into the midst of the fire? They answered and said unto the king, True, O king.* **25** *He answered and said, Lo, I see four men loose, walking in the midst of the fire, and they have no hurt; and the form of the fourth is like the Son of God.*

"Four men, loose, walking in the fire! I know we threw three in there. You know we threw three in there. Why is there a fourth man in there, and why isn't everyone in there dead? My best soldiers are dead, just from throwing them in, yet there are four people alive, walking around in that fire. And that fourth one isn't normal. He is not even human. That fourth one, even through the fire I can see that He is like the Son of God!"

Daniel 3:26 *Then Nebuchadnezzar came near to the mouth of the burning fiery furnace, and spake, and said,*

Shadrach, Meshach, and Abednego, ye servants of the most high God, come forth, and come hither. Then Shadrach, Meshach, and Abednego, came forth of the midst of the fire.

I am struck by several things right here. One, Nebuchadnezzar did not let these boys out; he called for them to come out. That means that they could have already come out if they had wanted to. Friends, walking with Jesus in the fire is better than walking without Him outside the fire!

Two, Nebuchadnezzar called for those three boys to come out, but did you notice that he did not call for that fourth one to come out? Nebuchadnezzar, who just a few minutes earlier had said, "Who is that God that shall deliver you out of my hands?" now all of a sudden was too scared to get near the God that did deliver them out of his hands. When God really moves in and does a work, mark it down that arrogant sinners will be scared to death to get near it.

Daniel 3:27 *And the princes, governors, and captains, and the king's counsellors, being gathered together, saw these men, upon whose bodies the fire had no power, nor was an hair of their head singed, neither were their coats changed, nor the smell of fire had passed on them.*

I love the way God does things. This was not done in secret; all of the governmental leaders in the kingdom saw it. They all clearly saw that there was no natural explanation. If it had somehow been a "natural phenomena," those boys would have at least smelled like smoke, their clothes would have at least been affected. But their clothes were like brand new, they did not have any odor of smoke, not one hair on their heads was singed, this was a pure and public miracle!

Daniel 3:28 *Then Nebuchadnezzar spake, and said, Blessed be the God of Shadrach, Meshach, and Abednego, who hath sent his angel, and delivered his servants that trusted in him, and have changed the king's word, and yielded their bodies, that they might not serve nor worship any god, except their own God.* **29** *Therefore I make a decree, That every people, nation, and language, which speak any thing amiss against the God of Shadrach, Meshach, and Abednego, shall*

69

be cut in pieces, and their houses shall be made a dunghill:
because there is no other God that can deliver after this sort.
30 *Then the king promoted Shadrach, Meshach, and*
Abednego, in the province of Babylon.

These boys loved God. Because of that, they did right.
They got thrown into the fire anyway. But God showed up, the
Fourth Man in the fire. They came out, and Nebuchadnezzar
made a decree that no one was allowed to speak anything amiss
against their God. Happy ending, except for one major thing:
Nebuchadnezzar still had a 90-foot idol standing outside, and
he did not tear it down. He just commanded that everyone be
respectful to the God of the Hebrews. That means that as
chapter three ends, Nebuchadnezzar the king is still lost.

Chapter 6
Broken

Daniel 4:1 *Nebuchadnezzar the king, unto all people, nations, and languages, that dwell in all the earth; Peace be multiplied unto you.* **2** *I thought it good to shew the signs and wonders that the high God hath wrought toward me.* **3** *How great are his signs! and how mighty are his wonders! his kingdom is an everlasting kingdom, and his dominion is from generation to generation.* **4** *I Nebuchadnezzar was at rest in mine house, and flourishing in my palace:* **5** *I saw a dream which made me afraid, and the thoughts upon my bed and the visions of my head troubled me.* **6** *Therefore made I a decree to bring in all the wise men of Babylon before me, that they might make known unto me the interpretation of the dream.* **7** *Then came in the magicians, the astrologers, the Chaldeans, and the soothsayers: and I told the dream before them; but they did not make known unto me the interpretation thereof.* **8** *But at the last Daniel came in before me, whose name was Belteshazzar, according to the name of my god, and in whom is the spirit of the holy gods: and before him I told the dream, saying,* **9** *O Belteshazzar, master of the magicians, because I know that the spirit of the holy gods is in thee, and no secret troubleth thee, tell me the visions of my dream that I have seen, and the interpretation thereof.* **10** *Thus were the visions of mine head in my bed; I saw, and behold a tree in the midst of the* *earth, and the height thereof was great.* **11** *The tree grew, and was strong, and the height thereof reached unto heaven, and the sight thereof to the end of all the earth:* **12** *The leaves thereof were fair, and the fruit thereof much, and in it was meat for all: the beasts of the field had shadow under it, and the fowls of the heaven dwelt in the boughs thereof, and all flesh was fed of it.* **13** *I saw in the visions of my head upon my bed, and, behold, a watcher and an holy one came down from heaven;* **14** *He cried aloud, and said thus, Hew down the tree, and cut off his branches, shake off his leaves, and scatter his fruit: let the beasts get away from under it, and the fowls from his branches:* **15** *Nevertheless leave the stump of his roots in the earth, even with a band of iron and brass, in the tender grass of the field; and let it be wet with the dew of heaven, and let his portion be with the beasts in the grass of the earth:* **16** *Let his heart be changed from man's, and let a beast's heart be given unto him; and let seven times pass over him.* **17** *This matter is by the decree of the watchers, and the demand by the word of the holy ones: to the intent that the living may know that the most High ruleth in the kingdom of men, and giveth it to whomsoever he will, and setteth up over it the basest of men.* **18** *This dream I king Nebuchadnezzar have seen. Now thou, O Belteshazzar, declare the interpretation thereof, forasmuch as all the wise men of my kingdom are not able to make known unto me the interpretation: but thou art able; for the spirit of the holy gods is in thee.* **19** *Then Daniel, whose name was Belteshazzar, was astonied for one hour, and his thoughts troubled him. The king spake, and said, Belteshazzar, let not the dream, or the interpretation thereof, trouble thee. Belteshazzar answered and said, My lord, the dream be to them that hate thee, and the interpretation thereof to thine enemies.* **20** *The tree that thou sawest, which grew, and was strong, whose height reached unto the heaven, and the sight thereof to all the earth;* **21** *Whose leaves were fair, and the fruit thereof much, and in it was meat for all; under which the beasts of the field dwelt, and upon whose branches the fowls of the heaven had their habitation:* **22** *It is thou, O king, that art grown and* *become strong: for thy greatness is grown, and reacheth unto heaven, and thy dominion to the end of the earth.* **23** *And whereas the king saw a watcher and an holy one coming down from heaven, and saying, Hew the tree down, and destroy it; yet leave the stump of the roots thereof in the earth, even with a band of iron and brass, in the tender grass of the field; and let it be wet with the dew of heaven, and let his portion be with the beasts of the field, till seven times pass over him;* **24** *This is the interpretation, O king, and this is the decree of the most High, which is come upon my lord the king:* **25** *That they shall drive thee from men, and thy dwelling shall be with the beasts of the field, and they shall make thee to eat grass as oxen, and they shall wet thee with the dew of heaven, and seven times shall pass over thee, till thou know that the most High ruleth in the kingdom of men, and giveth it to whomsoever he will.* **26** *And whereas they commanded to leave the stump of the tree roots; thy kingdom shall be sure unto thee, after that thou shalt have known that the heavens do rule.* **27** *Wherefore, O king, let my counsel be acceptable unto thee, and break off thy sins by righteousness, and thine iniquities by shewing mercy to the poor; if it may be a lengthening of thy tranquillity.* **28** *All this came upon the king Nebuchadnezzar.* **29** *At the end of twelve months he walked in the palace of the kingdom of Babylon.* **30** *The king spake, and said, Is not this great Babylon, that I have built for the house of the kingdom by the might of my power, and for the honour of my majesty?* **31** *While the word was in the king's mouth, there fell a voice from heaven, saying, O king Nebuchadnezzar, to thee it is spoken; The kingdom is departed from thee.* **32** *And they shall drive thee from men, and thy dwelling shall be with the beasts of the field: they shall make thee to eat grass as oxen, and seven times shall pass over thee, until thou know that the most High ruleth in the kingdom of men, and giveth it to whomsoever he will.* **33** *The same hour was the thing fulfilled upon Nebuchadnezzar: and he was driven from men, and did eat grass as oxen, and his body was wet with the dew of heaven, till his hairs were grown like eagles' feathers, and his nails like birds' claws.* **34** *And at the* *end of the days I Nebuchadnezzar lifted up mine eyes unto heaven, and mine understanding returned unto me, and I blessed the most High, and I praised and honoured him that liveth for ever, whose dominion is an everlasting dominion, and his kingdom is from generation to generation:* **35** *And all the inhabitants of the earth are reputed as nothing: and he doeth according to his will in the army of heaven, and among the inhabitants of the earth: and none can stay his hand, or say unto him, What doest thou?* **36** *At the same time my reason returned unto me; and for the glory of my kingdom, mine honour and brightness returned unto me; and my counsellors and my lords sought unto me; and I was established in my kingdom, and excellent majesty was added unto me.* **37** *Now I Nebuchadnezzar praise and extol and honour the King of heaven, all whose works are truth, and his ways judgment: and those that walk in pride he is able to abase.*

In all of our chapters thus far, we have really become acquainted with the heroes of the book – Daniel, Shadrach, Meshach, and Abednego. It almost feels like we know them personally. But in chapter four, we are going to get to know the villain of the book. And you might be amazed at how your feelings for him change from the beginning of the chapter to the end of the chapter.

A Heavenly Warning

Daniel 4:1 *Nebuchadnezzar the king, unto all people, nations, and languages, that dwell in all the earth; Peace be multiplied unto you.* **2** *I thought it good to shew the signs and wonders that the high God hath wrought toward me.* **3** *How great are his signs! and how mighty are his wonders! his kingdom is an everlasting kingdom, and his dominion is from generation to generation.*

Let me give you a little sense of perspective on what we just read. This is a letter from Nebuchadnezzar that he sent out to his entire world-wide kingdom. Listen to this letter, and then think of your reaction to it:

74

Bill Clinton, the former president, to whom it may concern, may God's blessings be upon you. I felt like it would be good to tell you what the great God, the Lord Jesus Christ, has done in my life. His Word, the King James Bible, is God's authoritative and inspired Word. His sacrifice on Calvary has given me forgiveness from my wretched, filthy sins. He is coming back soon to this wicked world, and I'll be caught up to meet him in the Rapture in the clouds. He shall reign forever and ever.

How surprised would you be to get that letter? Your reaction to that letter is probably about how everyone else felt to get a letter from Nebuchadnezzar that began like verses one through three. It is clear that something happened to Nebuchadnezzar, and the rest of the chapter will explain it.

Daniel 4:4 *I Nebuchadnezzar was at rest in mine house, and flourishing in my palace:* **5** *I saw a dream which made me afraid, and the thoughts upon my bed and the visions of my head troubled me.*

This is the second time that Nebuchadnezzar has had a dream that scared him to death. And truthfully, he had every right to be scared of this one as we will soon see.

Daniel 4:6 *Therefore made I a decree to bring in all the wise men of Babylon before me, that they might make known unto me the interpretation of the dream.* **7** *Then came in the magicians, the astrologers, the Chaldeans, and the soothsayers: and I told the dream before them; but they did not make known unto me the interpretation thereof.*

You will notice that Nebuchadnezzar handled things a bit differently this time than he did the first time. Earlier he demanded that the wise men of Babylon tell him the dream and the interpretation. This time he is so shaken up that he tells them the dream. He just wants to know what it means. But just like before, these guys are worthless. They are nothing more than palm-readers and astrologers. They cannot tell Nebuchadnezzar what the dream means. People like this have always been worthless. Never ever waste your money or your time on them.

Daniel 4:8 *But at the last Daniel came in before me, whose name was Belteshazzar, according to the name of my god, and in whom is the spirit of the holy gods: and before him I told the dream, saying,* **9** *O Belteshazzar, master of the magicians, because I know that the spirit of the holy gods is in thee, and no secret troubleth thee, tell me the visions of my dream that I have seen, and the interpretation thereof.*

You know what words are a shame in this verse? *At the last.* Daniel, the man of God, the man that had already proven that he could give the right answer, is again the last man to be called in a serious situation. But finally he was called, and Nebuchadnezzar told him the dream and asked for the interpretation.

Daniel 4:10 *Thus were the visions of mine head in my bed; I saw, and behold a tree in the midst of the earth, and the height thereof was great.* **11** *The tree grew, and was strong, and the height thereof reached unto heaven, and the sight thereof to the end of all the earth:* **12** *The leaves thereof were fair, and the fruit thereof much, and in it was meat for all: the beasts of the field had shadow under it, and the fowls of the heaven dwelt in the boughs thereof, and all flesh was fed of it.*

Here is the first part of the dream. Look at the particulars, and see if you can decipher it. The dream is about a tree in the very middle of the earth. In other words, it is the center, and everything else revolves around it, all the nations and peoples of the earth look to it. The tree is tall, strong, powerful, and can be seen and known from everywhere. The leaves are beautiful; it is a gorgeous tree to look at. It produces an amazing amount of fruit; people are nourished by it. It has a huge crest which produces shade and comfort. This is an unbelievable and impressive tree, something no one would ever forget. That is what makes this next part of the dream so frightening:

Daniel 4:13 *I saw in the visions of my head upon my bed, and, behold, a watcher and an holy one came down from heaven;* **14** *He cried aloud, and said thus, Hew down the tree, and cut off his branches, shake off his leaves, and scatter his* *fruit: let the beasts get away from under it, and the fowls from his branches:*

Nebuchadnezzar saw in his dream two angels come down from Heaven. One was an observer who would make a decision about the tree. The other was a holy one, an "executor of judgment" if you will. The first angel looks at the tree for a moment and then positively rips the air with a shout: ***Hew down the tree, and cut off his branches, shake off his leaves, and scatter his fruit: let the beasts get away from under it, and the fowls from his branches...***

The tree, whatever or whoever it was, was going to be cut down, de-leaved, fruit scattered, and all the animals were going to run from it like scalded dogs.

Daniel 4:15 *Nevertheless leave the stump of his roots in the earth, even with a band of iron and brass, in the tender grass of the field; and let it be wet with the dew of heaven, and let his portion be with the beasts in the grass of the earth:*

When we bought the land for the new church, that hillside had trees on it, completely obstructing the gorgeous view. So we had them cut down. But we did more than that. I got an excavator and spent countless hours, sometimes working well past midnight with the headlights of the machine, digging up all of those stumps. Then I left them out in piles where they dried up. Those trees are not growing back, ever.

In the dream of Nebuchadnezzar, the angel commanded to leave the stump in the earth. He then had a band of iron and brass put around it to protect it from injury. It was to be kept moist and watered while it was out in the field with the beasts. In other words, though that tree would never again be what it once was, it was at least possible that it might grow back again. But that encouraging turn was about to vanish quickly, as Nebuchadnezzar heard the next words from the angel:

Daniel 4:16 *Let his heart* (**not its heart, his heart**) *be changed from man's, and let a beast's heart be given unto him; and let seven times* (**a time is a year, so this is seven years we are talking about**) *pass over him.* **17** *This matter is by the decree of the watchers, and the demand by the word of the holy*

77

ones: to the intent that the living may know that the most High ruleth in the kingdom of men, and giveth it to whomsoever he will, and setteth up over it the basest of men.

Nebuchadnezzar knows now that this tree is a man, and something awful is about to happen to that man...

Daniel 4:18 *This dream I king Nebuchadnezzar have seen. Now thou, O Belteshazzar, declare the interpretation thereof, forasmuch as all the wise men of my kingdom are not able to make known unto me the interpretation: but thou art able; for the spirit of the holy gods is in thee.*

You can almost hear Nebuchadnezzar crying out: "Help me, Daniel. My wise men couldn't help me, but you can help me. Tell me what this dream means..."

Daniel 4:19 *Then Daniel, whose name was Belteshazzar, was astonied for one hour, and his thoughts troubled him. The king spake, and said, Belteshazzar, let not the dream, or the interpretation thereof, trouble thee. Belteshazzar answered and said, My lord, the dream be to them that hate thee, and the interpretation thereof to thine enemies.*

Daniel did not have to try and figure out the dream; he knew instantly what it meant. And for one hour, Daniel was so stunned that he could not even speak. Now imagine how scary that was for Nebuchadnezzar! The man who is going to tell him the dream, the man who in verse nine he described as a man that "nothing troubled him," that man is stunned speechless.

After an hour, Nebuchadnezzar himself spoke. He knew that Daniel was scared, and the king reached out to him and told him it would be OK, not to be afraid. The problem is, it was not going to be OK. I think Nebuchadnezzar figured that out pretty quickly when Daniel finally spoke and said, ***My lord, the dream be to them that hate thee, and the interpretation thereof to thine enemies.***

Daniel 4:20 *The tree that thou sawest, which grew, and was strong, whose height reached unto the heaven, and the sight thereof to all the earth;* **21** *Whose leaves were fair, and the fruit thereof much, and in it was meat for all; under which* *the beasts of the field dwelt, and upon whose branches the fowls of the heaven had their habitation: 22 It is thou, O king, that art grown and become strong: for thy greatness is grown, and reacheth unto heaven, and thy dominion to the end of the earth.*

It is thou, O King! Under ordinary circumstances, who would not want to be described as a tree like this? But Nebuchadnezzar remembered how that dream ended.

Daniel 4:23 *And whereas the king saw a watcher and an holy one coming down from heaven, and saying, Hew the tree down, and destroy it; yet leave the stump of the roots thereof in the earth, even with a band of iron and brass, in the tender grass of the field; and let it be wet with the dew of heaven, and let his portion be with the beasts of the field, till seven times pass over him; 24 This is the interpretation, O king, and this is the decree of the most High, which is come upon my lord the king: 25 That they shall drive thee from men, and thy dwelling shall be with the beasts of the field, and they shall make thee to eat grass as oxen, and they shall wet thee with the dew of heaven, and seven times shall pass over thee, till thou know that the most High ruleth in the kingdom of men, and giveth it to whomsoever he will. 26 And whereas they commanded to leave the stump of the tree roots; thy kingdom shall be sure unto thee, after that thou shalt have known that the heavens do rule.*

Imagine Nebuchadnezzar's horror and disbelief as he heard the verdict of God given by Daniel. Nebuchadnezzar was going to be driven out of the palace. His own subjects, his own court, were going to chase him out like a rabid animal, because he was suddenly going to start acting like a rabid animal. This all-powerful human king was going to become less than a human. Where he used to walk upright, tall, and proud, he was now going to crawl on all fours through the open fields. Where he once had enjoyed multiple luxurious meals every day, Nebuchadnezzar was going to spend seven years lowering his face to the ground and eating grass like the cattle of the field. When night fell, the King of Babylon would find some corner of the pasture and curl up on the ground to sleep. He would get soaked with the dew during the night and his own sweat during the day. He would not bathe or change clothes, and he would be like this for seven solid years.

There has never been a human being that fell farther than Nebuchadnezzar. He reached higher in human power than any other man and then fell lower than any human before or since. He literally went from one extreme end of the spectrum to the other, from the highest earthly heaven to the lowest earthly hell. And do you know why? Here is how Daniel put it at the end of verse twenty-five:

...till thou know that the most High ruleth in the kingdom of men, and giveth it to whomsoever he will.

Nebuchadnezzar did not know, or rather *would not know* the most obvious of truths: God is in charge, and He can give power or take it away at a moments notice. No king rules for one second longer than God wills. Humanity needs to learn this. No one lives for a moment longer than God wills. No one keeps their health or strength for a moment longer than God wills. No one retains a position for a moment longer than God wills. If we really knew how utterly dependant we are on God, it would humble us down to a proper level. And the higher a person has risen, the more they ought to have the sense to see and understand that they would not have gotten to where they have gotten without the sovereign God of Heaven.

Nebuchadnezzar should have gotten this. Daniel wanted him to get it. This young man, who had been taken as a slave from a foreign land by the man whose dream he was now interpreting, actually cared for this wicked king. He did not just give Nebuchadnezzar the message; he also proposed a possible solution:

Daniel 4:27 *Wherefore, O king, let my counsel be acceptable unto thee, and break off thy sins by righteousness, and thine iniquities by shewing mercy to the poor; if it may be a lengthening of thy tranquillity.*

Everyone likes things to be all black and white; "Here is the problem, here is the solution, done." Unfortunately, sin does not always leave things so easy to fix. There are some times that people come to me for counsel, and their sin has wreaked havoc in their lives, and so many things are broken beyond repair that the best solution I can give them is to point out the least bad of the bad options that they do have. Beware of sin; it often does that to you.

Daniel found himself looking at a man, a king, who was in a situation like that. Daniel did not have any hard and fast solutions for the problem that Nebuchadnezzar had caused himself. Daniel said, "Nebuchadnezzar, you need to do right, which you have not been doing up until now. You need to be merciful to the poor, which you have not been doing up until now. And Nebuchadnezzar, if you think enough of the God of Heaven to do these things I'm suggesting, **it may be** a lengthening of thy tranquility."

Daniel could not look Nebuchadnezzar in the eyes and say, "This will keep the judgment of God from falling on you." All he could say was, "Maybe, just maybe, God will show mercy to you if you do right."

How low has a person gotten when the best a man of God can offer is, "Start doing right this very minute and maybe God will briefly delay hammering you into the ground." It is a dangerous thing to well up in pride against God, go your own way, and do your own thing.

You may be in the same situation as King Nebuchadnezzar. You may have rebelled and sinned and sinned and rebelled and now it is obvious to you that you are facing the imminent judgment of God. Take my advice: do right, repent, and God *may* show mercy to you. You say, "Preacher, why should I do right just on the hope that God *may* show mercy to me?" For two reasons. First, a slight hope is a lot better than no hope. But second, if you are going to face the judgment of God anyway, you may as well do so with a clear conscience. At least that way you can get some sleep at night and not be ashamed to look yourself in the eyes in the mirror the next morning.

I was at the hospital with a church member in July of 2007 as he had surgery. When I sat down in the waiting room, I looked over and noticed that I was sitting beside a young guy in a drab white prison outfit, shackled hand and foot, with a guard standing just a few feet away. So I struck up a conversation with the young man. I asked him his name, and he said it was Kenny. I said, "Kenny, you're awful young; what are you in for?"

He said, "A car that they say I stole that I didn't steal. It's alright; I'll be out in a couple of weeks. That's when I go to court so they can find me innocent."

I looked at those shackled hands and feet... and then I looked at the police officer who was standing by listening. Now, I am an excellent reader. I read my Bible through from cover to cover for the first time when I was nine years old. But you know what I can read just about as good? Faces. That officer's face may as well have been inscribed in indelible ink. That look said *Oh, brother! If this perpetual troublemaker thinks anyone in the world is going to buy this 'innocent act,' he has another thing coming*! When we left, I told my wife, "That boy is going away for a very long time."

And you know what? If he is as guilty as I suspect he is, he is going to undergo the judgment of the law and have his own guilty conscience to deal with at the same time. That is a bad plan! If you are doing wrong, you need to quit. I can't promise that God will pull back the spanking He has planned for you, but I can tell you that *He might.* I can also tell you that you will enjoy life a lot more, even under the judgment of God, if you have a clear conscience.

A Hellish Pride
Daniel 4:28 *All this came upon the king Nebuchadnezzar.*

There is not one doubt in my mind that Nebuchadnezzar thought he would get by. Like so many people, he thought he could sin and win. And the fact that judgment did not fall immediately helped him to feel that way.

But from the moment judgment was pronounced, God started the clock ticking down, and that clock was set for exactly one year.

Daniel 4:29 *At the end of twelve months he walked in the palace of the kingdom of Babylon.* **30** *The king spake, and said, Is not this great Babylon, that I have built for the house of the kingdom by the might of my power, and for the honour of my majesty?*

Nebuchadnezzar was dead right when he called it *Great Babylon.* There has not before or since been a city quite like it. Babylon was roughly the size of Houston, Texas, and had a population of more than a million people. Around the city there was an inner wall built, 350 feet high, 87 feet thick. A half mile further out, there was another wall built the exact same size. That made for 30 square miles of rich crop land in between. On top of the walls were 250 watchtowers, 450 feet high. Running around the wall was a deep water moat, 30 feet wide. Filling the moat and running underneath the walls into and through the city was the Euphrates River. So this city had all of the food and water needed for any length of a siege, and walls to protect them from any enemy.

The architecture was just as impressive as the fortifications. The hanging gardens, basically an artificial mountain built for one of his homesick wives, was one of the seven ancient wonders of the world. This was a great city!

Here are the two problems with what Nebuchadnezzar said. First of all, he did not build it. It had been around long before his day. He did help to make it great, but he did not build it. He just gave commands, and his laborers did the actual work of making it great.

Secondly, Nebuchadnezzar was all caught up in his own magnificence when the clock of God's judgment was ticking against him. He should have had his face on the ground, begging for the mercy of God, but instead, he had his nose in the air, bragging about how great he was. Nebuchadnezzar was inflicted with and infested by hellish pride. When a person does wrong, gets warned about what is

83

going to happen, and keeps right on doing wrong anyway, it is pride! And it will cost you!

During the Battle of the Wilderness in the Civil War, Union General John Sedgwick was inspecting his troops. At one point he came to a parapet, over which he gazed out in the direction of the enemy. His officers suggested that this was unwise and perhaps he ought to duck while passing the parapet. "Nonsense," snapped the general. "They couldn't hit an elephant at this dist--." A moment later Sedgwick fell to the ground, fatally wounded. Beware of pride; it will cost you!

A Humbling Judgment

Daniel 4:31 *While the word was in the king's mouth, there fell a voice from heaven, saying, O king Nebuchadnezzar, to thee it is spoken; The kingdom is departed from thee. 32 And they shall drive thee from men, and thy dwelling shall be with the beasts of the field: they shall make thee to eat grass as oxen, and seven times shall pass over thee, until thou know that the most High ruleth in the kingdom of men, and giveth it to whomsoever he will.*

While Nebuchadnezzar was uttering the word "majesty," Majesty Himself spoke. Time was up. Nebuchadnezzar heard God speak out loud from the heavens and tell him that he had lost the kingdom and was going to live like an animal until he developed enough sense to know that God was in charge.

Daniel 4:33 *The same hour was the thing fulfilled upon Nebuchadnezzar: and he was driven from men, and did eat grass as oxen, and his body was wet with the dew of heaven, till his hairs were grown like eagles' feathers, and his nails like birds' claws.*

Just put yourself there, in the palace of Babylon, and imagine what this was like. Nebuchadnezzar, greatest of all human kings, stricken with insanity and driven out as a beast!

Daniel 4:34 *And at the end of the days I Nebuchadnezzar lifted up mine eyes unto heaven, and mine understanding returned unto me, and I blessed the most High,* *and I praised and honoured him that liveth for ever, whose dominion is an everlasting dominion, and his kingdom is from generation to generation:* **35** *And all the inhabitants of the earth are reputed as nothing: and he doeth according to his will in the army of heaven, and among the inhabitants of the earth: and none can stay his hand, or say unto him, What doest thou?* **36** *At the same time my reason returned unto me; and for the glory of my kingdom, mine honour and brightness returned unto me; and my counsellors and my lords sought unto me; and I was established in my kingdom, and excellent majesty was added unto me.*

Please notice that this was simultaneous. The moment that Nebuchadnezzar finally broke, God restored him. Dwell on that for a moment. The moment that Nebuchadnezzar finally broke, God restored him! It is so frustrating seeing sinners struggle and get hammered and struggle and be miserable when all they have to do is finally break, finally give in, and surrender to God.

Look at what Nebuchadnezzar said that shows what he finally learned:

Daniel 4:34 *... I blessed the most High, and I praised and honoured him that liveth for ever, whose dominion is an everlasting dominion, and his kingdom is from generation to generation:* **35** *And all the inhabitants of the earth are reputed as nothing: and he doeth according to his will in the army of heaven, and among the inhabitants of the earth: and none can stay his hand, or say unto him, What doest thou?*

And then look at the result:

Daniel 4:36 *At the same time my reason returned unto me; and for the glory of my kingdom, mine honour and brightness returned unto me; and my counsellors and my lords sought unto me; and I was established in my kingdom, and excellent majesty was added unto me.*

You can thank Daniel for this, he knew when the seven years was up!

Daniel 4:37 *Now I Nebuchadnezzar praise and extol and honour the King of heaven, all whose works are truth, and* *his ways judgment: and those that walk in pride he is able to abase.*

If ever a man of pride was broken, it was Nebuchadnezzar. God be praised that He gave that prideful man a chance to be restored!

Chapter 7
In That Night

Thus far in this book I have printed the entire chapter and then gone through it. In this chapter, I just want to show the next to the last verse, and then we will go back to the beginning and work our way through the entire chapter.

Daniel 5:30 *In that night was Belshazzar the king of the Chaldeans slain.*

If you have paid attention at all, you know that the word *Breathtaking* perfectly describes this book. The siege and captivity, the test that Daniel and his friends passed by not partaking of the king's wine and meat, the nightmare of Nebuchadnezzar, the fiery furnace, the seven years where Nebuchadnezzar was reduced to living like an animal in the open field, this book is fast and furious! Chapter five is no exception. The very last thing we read was about Nebuchadnezzar becoming like a beast and then getting saved, and then, in the very next verse, we are back in another tense, high-pressure situation, this time under the very last king of the Chaldeans, a man named Belshazzar.

Chapter four covered more than eight years in rapid-fire style. Chapter five covers just one night, one night that had enough action for eight years.

In That Night, Belshazzar Threw a Fling

Daniel 5:1 *Belshazzar the king made a great feast to a thousand of his lords, and drank wine before the thousand.*

As you get to the very first verse, you know right away that some things have changed in Babylon. Nebuchadnezzar had been dead for nearly 30 years. His son Nabonidus was the king, but he was away in Arabia. The people did not mind, because nobody liked him. He was a terrible king with no leadership abilities. Nabonidus' son was the co-regent and was on the throne in his father's absence. His name was Belshazzar, and the year was 539 B.C.

Belshazzar, in that night, threw himself and a few thousand of his buddies a fling. He got roaring, falling-down drunk and did so where all of those thousands could see him. But that was not enough for him. It did not make him a "big enough man" to all of these people he wanted to impress. So he went a step farther:

Daniel 5:2 *Belshazzar, whiles he tasted the wine, commanded to bring the golden and silver vessels which his father Nebuchadnezzar had taken out of the temple which was in Jerusalem; that the king, and his princes, his wives, and his concubines, might drink therein.* **3** *Then they brought the golden vessels that were taken out of the temple of the house of God which was at Jerusalem; and the king, and his princes, his wives, and his concubines, drank in them.*

Mr. Belshazzar was buzzing from wine. Trying to find a way to make a bigger impression, he thought back to some things that were in the treasury. There were some golden and silver vessels that had been taken out of the Temple in Jerusalem decades earlier. If you remember much about the first five books of the Bible, those vessels were used in the sacrifices and feasts and worship to Jehovah God. Those vessels were sacred; they were holy. Belshazzar commanded those vessels to be brought out. They passed them around and poured booze, liquor, the liquid fruit of Hell itself, into those sacred vessels. Then they raised those vessels to their polluted lips and chugged away. But even that was not enough for Belshazzar:

Daniel 5:4 *They drank wine, and praised the gods of gold, and of silver, of brass, of iron, of wood, and of stone.*

Drunkenness wasn't enough. Defiling those sacred vessels wasn't enough. Belshazzar had to go and add insult to injury by mocking the true and living God. Belshazzar said, "Hey! You people pay attention. Those Jews think their 'Living God' is real. If He is, why am I drinking out of His stuff? Let me tell you why. He isn't real. **Our** gods that we have made with **our** hands out of **our** gold and **our** silver and **our** brass and **our** iron and wood and stone, they're the real gods around here. Everybody drink up! A toast to our gods! "

Belshazzar was living it up! Man, what a party. Thousands of people in attendance, this was the bash of the century! You can see Belshazzar there on the throne, cheesy drunken grin on his plastered face. That's the close up mental camera view we have. But pull the camera out a ways. Now you can see the entire palace courtyard, teeming with dumb drunks. Pull out even farther, and now you can see the elaborate streets and architecture in the city around the palace. Pull out even father, and you can see the homes and businesses that stretch out to the city's edge, with only a few lights still left on for the night. Pull out one more time, just a bit farther, and let me tell you what you would see this time, if you had been there in that night: the entire city was surrounded by the armies of the Medo-Persian Empire. Thousands upon thousands of brutal soldiers with swords, spears, bows and arrows, determined to get into that city.

Here is what is so surprising: Belshazzar the king knew that they were out there. He just did not care! His big party was his way of thumbing his nose at the enemy and saying, "You and God put together can't get you in here, so hey, here's a toast to you, suckers!"

Here is why Belshazzar was acting like such a fool, partying while the enemy was trying to beat down the doors: Babylon was the most secure city of all times. If you remember, in the last chapter we learned that it had an inner wall 350 feet high and 87 feet thick and an outer wall half a mile away the exact same size. In between those two walls was 30 square miles of crop land for growing food. There was a mote, 30 feet wide and 30 feet deep fed by the Euphrates River surrounding the entire city and then running under the wall and through the city. Belshazzar figured that there was no army, no man, no God that could take him down while he was partying hard inside this great city.

So in that night, Belshazzar threw a fling. But that is not the end of the story.

In That Night, Bravado Gave Way to Fear

I love the way God does things:

Daniel 5:5 *In the same hour came forth fingers of a man's hand, and wrote over against the candlestick upon the plaister of the wall of the king's palace: and the king saw the part of the hand that wrote.*

Do your best to let this sink in as if you were there, as if you were Belshazzar. You are drinking and partying, laughing and living it up. You are letting everybody know that those great big armies outside do not scare you. But then all of the sudden your eyes catch sight of something small. A floating hand, with no arm or body attached to it. It is calmly writing on your wall.

The text tells us that there were ladies (wives and concubines) there. I wonder what the pandemonium was like when one of them saw it and screamed like a Banshee. Party time over.

Daniel 5:6 *Then the king's countenance was changed, and his thoughts troubled him, so that the joints of his loins were loosed, and his knees smote one against another.*

Have you ever heard of someone being so scared that their knees knocked together? That literally happened to Belshazzar. I am not trying to be inappropriate, but the truth is that Mr. Party Boy/King is so scared he is literally about to wet himself.

90

Daniel 5:7 *The king cried aloud to bring in the astrologers, the Chaldeans, and the soothsayers. And the king spake, and said to the wise men of Babylon, Whosoever shall read this writing, and shew me the interpretation thereof, shall be clothed with scarlet, and have a chain of gold about his neck, and shall be the third ruler in the kingdom.*

Notice that Belshazzar could only offer the third ruling position in the kingdom, because he was only the second man in the kingdom himself. But here he is, scared to death, wailing for his Chaldean wise men to come bail him out. This man had learned nothing from his forefathers.

Daniel 5:8 *Then came in all the king's wise men: but they could not read the writing, nor make known to the king the interpretation thereof.*

Worthless. These wise men were absolutely worthless. They were batting zero for their career and still had jobs. They must have had the best union in the history of organized labor.

Daniel 5:9 *Then was king Belshazzar greatly troubled, and his countenance was changed in him, and his lords were astonied.*

Belshazzar was torn up. First by what he saw, and secondly by the fact that no one could tell him what it meant. He was so upset, in fact, that his people were more amazed at him than they were at the floating/writing hand!

Daniel 5:10 *Now the queen, by reason of the words of the king and his lords, came into the banquet house: and the queen spake and said, O king, live for ever: let not thy thoughts trouble thee, nor let thy countenance be changed:*

There is a fact in this verse that makes it all the more beautiful. Commentators and historians tell us that this queen spoken of here was queen Amiyt, the widow of Nebuchadnezzar.[2] This old woman was at home, avoiding all the revelry. Her husband had gotten saved years before, after seven years out in the field. The man responsible for her husband getting saved was still alive, a man named Daniel.

Daniel has avoided the party. Amiyt has avoided the party. But when she hears the commotion, the screaming, the pandemonium, and then hears what the king is saying, she gets up, heads for her door. She makes her way through the streets and barges into the palace where her husband used to be king, where Daniel used to be a trusted advisor. Things have changed a lot. A whole lot. Belshazzar is a petty, spoiled little man, where her husband even when he was lost at least used to be a real man. Daniel is no longer an advisor, let alone a trusted advisor. He is an old man up in his eighties and has been pushed off to the side and forgotten about. But the queen had not forgotten:

Daniel 5:11 *There is a man in thy kingdom, in whom is the spirit of the holy gods; and in the days of thy father light and understanding and wisdom, like the wisdom of the gods, was found in him; whom the king Nebuchadnezzar thy father, the king, I say, thy father, made master of the magicians, astrologers, Chaldeans, and soothsayers;* **12** *Forasmuch as an excellent spirit, and knowledge, and understanding, interpreting of dreams, and shewing of hard sentences, and dissolving of doubts, were found in the same Daniel, whom the king named Belteshazzar: now let Daniel be called, and he will shew the interpretation.*

I love that the queen had not forgotten the man who led her husband to the Lord. I love that she remembered his skill and his walk with God. I love that she still had confidence in him even though he was eighty-plus years old. The queen said, "Sonny, you call Daniel. Daniel can answer your questions for you."

Daniel 5:13 *Then was Daniel brought in before the king. And the king spake and said unto Daniel, Art thou that Daniel, which art of the children of the captivity of Judah, whom the king my father brought out of Jewry?* **14** *I have even heard of thee, that the spirit of the gods is in thee, and that light and understanding and excellent wisdom is found in thee.* **15** *And now the wise men, the astrologers, have been brought in before me, that they should read this writing, and make known unto me the interpretation thereof: but they could not shew the interpretation of the thing:* **16** *And I have heard of thee, that*

92

thou canst make interpretations, and dissolve doubts: now if thou canst read the writing, and make known to me the interpretation thereof, thou shalt be clothed with scarlet, and have a chain of gold about thy neck, and shalt be the third ruler in the kingdom.

What a bargain: Daniel, I've desecrated the vessels from the Temple of your God. I've worshiped gods of metal and wood and mocked Jehovah. I've brought my kingdom to the point of ruin, the armies of the Medes and Persians are outside the gate, they're probably going to storm in here and kill all of the rulers at any minute. Daniel, if you tell me what the writing means, I'll make you one of the highest rulers in this kingdom, so you can be killed too.

Who could ask for anything more?

Daniel 5:17 *Then Daniel answered and said before the king, Let thy gifts be to thyself, and give thy rewards to another; yet I will read the writing unto the king, and make known to him the interpretation.*

If you do not want a sharp, harsh answer on something, you might not ought to ask an old crotchety preacher who ran out of patience years ago. Daniel is offered these gifts and these rewards. Most people would drool all over that opportunity. Daniel says, "Give my gifts back to yourself, give the rewards to one of your buddies, I don't need squat from you. But hang onto your paper crown, big boy, because I'm gonna tell you what the writing means anyway..."

And then, hardly taking a breath, Daniel launches:

Daniel 5:18 *O thou king, the most high God gave Nebuchadnezzar thy father a kingdom, and majesty, and glory, and honour:* **19** *And for the majesty that he gave him, all people, nations, and languages, trembled and feared before him: whom he would he slew; and whom he would he kept alive; and whom he would he set up; and whom he would he put down.* **20** *But when his heart was lifted up, and his mind hardened in pride, he was deposed from his kingly throne, and they took his glory from him:* **21** *And he was driven from the sons of men; and his heart was made like the beasts, and his*

93

dwelling was with the wild asses: they fed him with grass like oxen, and his body was wet with the dew of heaven; till he knew that the most high God ruled in the kingdom of men, and that he appointeth over it whomsoever he will. 22 And thou his son, O Belshazzar, hast not humbled thine heart, though thou knewest all this; 23 But hast lifted up thyself against the Lord of heaven; and they have brought the vessels of his house before thee, and thou, and thy lords, thy wives, and thy concubines, have drunk wine in them; and thou hast praised the gods of silver, and gold, of brass, iron, wood, and stone, which see not, nor hear, nor know: and the God in whose hand thy breath is, and whose are all thy ways, hast thou not glorified:

Daniel...is...HOT! He has had it up to here with this punk of a king, and he does not care if his head is chopped off this very night, he is going to go ballistic on this reprobate no matter what. But the sentence is not over yet. There is a colon at the end of verse twenty-three; Daniel still has not taken a breath:

Daniel 5:24 *Then was the part of the hand sent from him; and this writing was written. 25 And this is the writing that was written, MENE, MENE, TEKEL, UPHARSIN.*

Do you remember where this was written? On the wall of the palace. Do you know what is so significant about that? Writing on the palace wall was a very common thing. Every king had his courtiers write all over the palace walls about how great of a king he was. Most of what we know about ancient kings we know from writing found on ancient walls. Belshazzar was used to looking at that wall and reading all kinds of glorious things about himself. He would doubtless spend hours at a time reading every glowing lie on that wall about himself.

But in that night, there were not sentences and paragraphs and chapters written, there were just four words: *mene, mene, tekel, upharsin.* Four words, but those four little words were going to wipe out whatever shred of bravado that Belshazzar still had left in him. And by the way, these words

94

show again how worthless the "wise men" were. They were written in words that could be understood both in Hebrew and Chaldaeic, and these guys were either too drunk or too dumb to notice.

Daniel 5:26 *This is the interpretation of the thing: MENE; God hath numbered thy kingdom, and finished it.*

That word mene appeared twice, and it means "numbered and finished". The fact that it appeared twice means it was a done deal. There was no chance that it could be stopped even if Belshazzar had repented right then and there in sackcloth and ashes.

Daniel 5:27 *TEKEL; Thou art weighed in the balances, and art found wanting.*

Tekel means "weighed" and "too light." God put Belshazzar on His Divine scales and found him to be light and worthless.

Daniel 5:28 *PERES; Thy kingdom is divided, and given to the Medes and Persians.*

Upharsin as verse twenty-five has it is the same word as Peres in verse twenty-eight. In Hebrew it means "Persians" and in Chaldee it means "divided and given to." Belshazzar, that is the handwriting on the wall. Your kingdom is done. You have been weighed in the balances and found wanting. You are going to fall this night to the Medes and the Persians. Belshazzar, turn out the lights, the party is over.

Daniel 5:29 *Then commanded Belshazzar, and they clothed Daniel with scarlet, and put a chain of gold about his neck, and made a proclamation concerning him, that he should be the third ruler in the kingdom.*

Belshazzar was either spiteful or stupid or both. He has just been told his kingdom is done, and here he is making Daniel the third ruler in the kingdom against his wishes.

In that night, Belshazzar threw a fling. In that night, bravado gave way to fear...

In That Night, Babylon Fell

Daniel 5:30 *In that night was Belshazzar the king of the Chaldeans slain.* **31** *And Darius the Median took the kingdom, being about threescore and two years old.*

What about the walls? What about the mote? What about the great Euphrates River? What about the Babylonian army? What happened? Here is what happened. First off, all of the leaders were stone drunk! No one who should have been paying attention was paying attention; people everywhere were too busy engaging in open acts of fornication and lewdness. They had become so engrossed in sin that they did not even notice the water level of the Euphrates River dropping. You see, the Medo-Persians had divided the army into three sections. One was at the far end of the city, where the water went back under the walls and back out into the desert. The second was at the near end of the city, where the water first went under the walls into the city. The third had gone several miles upstream and dug a channel that they opened up to divert some of the flow of the river. So as the water level fell, the armies simply marched under the walls from both sides.[3]

But even once under the walls, it may have taken them considerable time to find Belshazzar in a city so large. But that was taken care of as well. You see, when the king is corrupt, you can expect that corruption to trickle down to lesser officials as well. Two Babylonian officers, Gadatas and Gobryas, had taken a bribe from the Medes and Persians. They were waiting there for the enemy. They opened everything up for the enemy and led the enemy armies right into the palace, where Belshazzar had just finished putting a gold chain around Daniel's neck.[4]

Can you imagine what it was like for Belshazzar to look up, see the armies of the enemy standing in front of him, and realize that he had gotten his own people so drunk that they couldn't protect him even if they wanted to? In that night, Belshazzar was slain. In that night, Belshazzar went to hell with beer on his breath. He never expected it. But then, no sinner ever expects that *this night* is actually *that night.*

Chapter 8
Of Loopholes and Lions

Daniel 6:1 *It pleased Darius to set over the kingdom an hundred and twenty princes, which should be over the whole kingdom;* **2** *And over these three presidents; of whom Daniel was first: that the princes might give accounts unto them, and the king should have no damage.* **3** *Then this Daniel was preferred above the presidents and princes, because an excellent spirit was in him; and the king thought to set him over the whole realm.* **4** *Then the presidents and princes sought to find occasion against Daniel concerning the kingdom; but they could find none occasion nor fault; forasmuch as he was faithful, neither was there any error or fault found in him.* **5** *Then said these men, We shall not find any occasion against this Daniel, except we find it against him concerning the law of his God.* **6** *Then these presidents and princes assembled together to the king, and said thus unto him, King Darius, live for ever.* **7** *All the presidents of the kingdom, the governors, and the princes, the counsellors, and the captains, have consulted together to establish a royal statute, and to make a firm decree, that whosoever shall ask a petition of any God or man for thirty days, save of thee, O king, he shall be cast into the den of lions.* **8** *Now, O king, establish the decree, and sign the writing, that it be not changed, according to the law of the Medes and Persians, which altereth not.* **9** *Wherefore king*

97

Darius signed the writing and the decree. **10** *Now when Daniel knew that the writing was signed, he went into his house; and his windows being open in his chamber toward Jerusalem, he kneeled upon his knees three times a day, and prayed, and gave thanks before his God, as he did aforetime.* **11** *Then these men assembled, and found Daniel praying and making supplication before his God.* **12** *Then they came near, and spake before the king concerning the king's decree; Hast thou not signed a decree, that every man that shall ask a petition of any God or man within thirty days, save of thee, O king, shall be cast into the den of lions? The king answered and said, The thing is true, according to the law of the Medes and Persians, which altereth not.* **13** *Then answered they and said before the king, That Daniel, which is of the children of the captivity of Judah, regardeth not thee, O king, nor the decree that thou hast signed, but maketh his petition three times a day.* **14** *Then the king, when he heard these words, was sore displeased with himself, and set his heart on Daniel to deliver him: and he laboured till the going down of the sun to deliver him.* **15** *Then these men assembled unto the king, and said unto the king, Know, O king, that the law of the Medes and Persians is, That no decree nor statute which the king establisheth may be changed.* **16** *Then the king commanded, and they brought Daniel, and cast him into the den of lions. Now the king spake and said unto Daniel, Thy God whom thou servest continually, he will deliver thee.* **17** *And a stone was brought, and laid upon the mouth of the den; and the king sealed it with his own signet, and with the signet of his lords; that the purpose might not be changed concerning Daniel.* **18** *Then the king went to his palace, and passed the night fasting: neither were instruments of musick brought before him: and his sleep went from him.* **19** *Then the king arose very early in the morning, and went in haste unto the den of lions.* **20** *And when he came to the den, he cried with a lamentable voice unto Daniel: and the king spake and said to Daniel, O Daniel, servant of the living God, is thy God, whom thou servest continually, able to deliver thee from the lions?* **21** *Then said Daniel unto the king, O king, live* *for ever.* **22** *My God hath sent his angel, and hath shut the lions' mouths, that they have not hurt me: forasmuch as before him innocency was found in me; and also before thee, O king, have I done no hurt.* **23** *Then was the king exceeding glad for him, and commanded that they should take Daniel up out of the den. So Daniel was taken up out of the den, and no manner of hurt was found upon him, because he believed in his God.* **24** *And the king commanded, and they brought those men which had accused Daniel, and they cast them into the den of lions, them, their children, and their wives; and the lions had the mastery of them, and brake all their bones in pieces or ever they came at the bottom of the den.* **25** *Then king Darius wrote unto all people, nations, and languages, that dwell in all the earth; Peace be multiplied unto you.* **26** *I make a decree, That in every dominion of my kingdom men tremble and fear before the God of Daniel: for he is the living God, and stedfast for ever, and his kingdom that which shall not be destroyed, and his dominion shall be even unto the end.* **27** *He delivereth and rescueth, and he worketh signs and wonders in heaven and in earth, who hath delivered Daniel from the power of the lions.* **28** *So this Daniel prospered in the reign of Darius, and in the reign of Cyrus the Persian.*

We have made our way through the first five chapters of the book of Daniel thus far. We have seen Daniel go from a boy who was taken prisoner into Babylon to a fiery old man who lived an entire life for God. We have seen Babylon go from a mighty nation knocking down the walls of Jerusalem to a nation that rotted from within and saw its own great walls breached by the Medes and the Persians. In these first five chapters we have encountered two nightmares, a fiery furnace, and a king that became an animal. One king has gotten saved; another has died and gone to hell. This book truly is *Breathtaking*.

And that brings us up to chapter six where a new kingdom is inside the glorious walls of Babylon, and a new king is on the throne.

A Different Order

Daniel 6:1 *It pleased Darius to set over the kingdom an hundred and twenty princes, which should be over the whole kingdom;* **2** *And over these three presidents; of whom Daniel was first: that the princes might give accounts unto them, and the king should have no damage.*

It only takes two verses of Daniel six for us to see that things have changed drastically in Babylon, especially since the days of Nebuchadnezzar. When Nebuchadnezzar was king, the only law was Nebuchadnezzar himself. He could do whatever he wanted, whenever he wanted to do it, and no one could stop him. But as the head of gold fell, the upper body of silver took over, and the entire order of things changed. Nebuchadnezzar ruled by himself. Darius and the Medo-Persian Empire used a hierarchal system of government. There were 120 provinces in their world-wide kingdom and by the time of Esther 1:1 they had added seven more provinces. Darius set up a prince over each of those provinces. Then he appointed a committee of three presidents that those 120 princes answered to. Among those three presidents, one was in charge over the other two and answered directly to the king.

The normal, customary thing to do would be for this new king to appoint as his closest advisors the men that he had grown to trust through the years. The last thing in the world any king would ever do is leave any of the old administration in place. They would be regarded as threats and were usually killed on the spot.

But not this time. Darius came into the kingdom just as Daniel was being rewarded by the king that Darius was about to kill. Daniel was made the third ruler in the fallen kingdom. There was not one reason in the world to keep him alive. So how did Daniel end up staying alive and then becoming the second ruler in the new kingdom? That is a highly unlikely occurrence. How did it happen here?

There is this thing that people spend their lives building; it is called a reputation. Whenever any kingdom goes to war against another, the first thing they do is learn everything there is to know about their enemy, especially the leaders they will be going against. Do you remember right after 9-11? Even before we went into Afghanistan there were pictures of Osama Bin Laden and every one of his lieutenants all over television. We were told where these guys were born, what they were like, right down to their personality traits. Same thing before we went into Iraq. We knew all about Saddam and Chemical Ali and Saddam's deadbeat sons, Ouday and Kousay.

The Medes and the Persians were no different. They did their homework. Before they ever got into that walled city, they knew all about the late, great king Nebuchadnezzar, pathetic Nabonidus, and party-boy Belshazzar. And knowing all of that, they could not have helped but learn about a godly old man named Daniel who had served under each one of those kings. Daniel did not think fast and talk slick to save his life. Daniel spent 70 years in Babylon building an excellent reputation, and that is what saved his life and caused Darius to put this Jewish captive as the second man in the kingdom.

Daniel 6:3 *Then this Daniel was preferred above the presidents and princes, because an excellent spirit was in him; and the king thought to set him over the whole realm.*

Daniel was made second in command based on his excellent reputation. But after serving in that capacity for a while, Darius got to see Daniel for himself and realized what a gem he had on his hands. As an old man, seventy years removed from home, he still has such an excellent spirit about him that Darius is thinking about basically turning the entire operations of the kingdom over to Daniel. Darius is going to be the king with the easiest job in the world; taking the credit while Daniel handles everything. And Daniel is about to be given the best promotion any foreign captive ever received since the days of Joseph!

Daniel 6:4 *Then the presidents and princes sought to find occasion against Daniel concerning the kingdom...*

These guys are eaten up with jealousy! 122 men are furious that a foreign slave has gotten this promotion instead of one of them, and they aren't going to put up with it. They decide to poke around in Daniel's private life, find out what skeletons are in his closet, and out him before the king so that Darius has to make Daniel step down and appoint one of them. But look at the last part of this verse:

*...but they could **find** none occasion nor fault; forasmuch as he was faithful, neither was there any error or fault **found** in him.*

I love this, and believe me, any preacher could preach on this one thought for months: they *looked for* something wrong and could not find it.

Let me put it in language we can understand for today: they followed him around from a distance to see where he went, and Daniel never went anywhere he shouldn't have. They logged onto his Facebook account and went through every page and every picture, and every bit of it was as pure as the wind-driven snow. They rifled through his checkbook, and all of his money was spent on non-sinful things. They poked around in his closet, and there were no immodest clothes. They found his diary, went through it page by page, and there was not one thing Daniel had to be embarrassed about. They checked his cell phone, read every text message, and there was not one bad word, not one hurtful comment about another person, not one evil insinuation.

How many of us would come through an examination like that as well as Daniel did? Listen to me: we should! Every one of us should. If we truly live for God, people should be able to poke around like crazy in our lives and come up totally frustrated because we live right in all things and there is nothing bad to find!

After an examination like that and seeing what kind of man Daniel was, it would seem like these men would back off. But evil doesn't work that way.

Daniel 6:5 *Then said these men, We shall not find any occasion against this Daniel, except we find it against him concerning the law of his God.*

These men were wicked, but they were very perceptive as well. They saw something in Daniel. They saw that his highest devotion was to God. He was more devoted to God than he was to family, friends, or even the king. They rightly reasoned that if there was ever a conflict between king and God, Daniel would side with God. But there was no conflict there. There was nothing in the law of God that made for any conflict in Daniel's loyalty to the king. So what did these men do? They decided to invent a conflict where there was none:

Daniel 6:6 *Then these presidents and princes assembled together to the king, and said thus unto him, King Darius, live for ever. 7 All the presidents of the kingdom, the governors, and the princes, the counsellors, and the captains, have consulted together to establish a royal statute, and to make a firm decree, that whosoever shall ask a petition of any God or man for thirty days, save of thee, O king, he shall be cast into the den of lions. 8 Now, O king, establish the decree, and sign the writing, that it be not changed, according to the law of the Medes and Persians, which altereth not.*

One hundred twenty-two men assembled together to speak to the king. It should have been 123, but Daniel was not invited to the party. These men assured the king that Daniel was with them on this. Notice what they said all the presidents and princes have agreed to this, "Daniel is with us, O King; he thinks this is a great idea! So here's the plan. You're the new king in town, and we need to get it firmly established that everyone looks to you. So for thirty days, make a decree that no one can ask for anything from anyone; not a man, not a god, no one but you. That will make everybody see how bad they need you and how great you are, O King. Oh and by the way, this proclamation needs to have some teeth to it. Decree that if anyone disobeys this, he gets cast into a den full of lions. And king, remember that once you sign it, it becomes Medo-Persian law and cannot be changed."

These men were playing to Darius' pride. They were also trying to get him not just to decree it verbally, but also to sign it into law. You see, where Nebuchadnezzar had been the law and could do anything or change anything anytime he wanted, the Medes and the Persians held to the written law. Their written law, once signed by the king, could not be changed even by the king himself. They wanted to make sure that once Daniel fell into their trap, there was no way he could be gotten out of it.

Daniel 6:9 *Wherefore king Darius signed the writing and the decree.*

Darius never stopped to consider the consequences of what he was doing. There was a different order in town, a new king on the throne, a new law on the books, and an old man with a decision to make.

A Determined Believer

Daniel 6:10 *Now when Daniel knew that the writing was signed, he went into his house; and his windows being open in his chamber toward Jerusalem, he kneeled upon his knees three times a day, and prayed, and gave thanks before his God, as he did aforetime.* **11** *Then these men assembled, and found Daniel praying and making supplication before his God.*

The news of what happened did not take long to get to Daniel, and he knew right away at whom this was aimed. So now he had some choices to make.

Option one, he could hold off praying for thirty days. Surely God would understand that he was only trying to save his life. But you see, Daniel would rather die than not talk to God, so that option was off the table for him just like it should be for us.

Option two, he could pray with the doors and the windows shut so no one would see. But then all those people that Daniel had witnessed to through the years would think, "If Daniel's God isn't any more important than that, if Daniel isn't praying anymore, why should we believe in Him?" So that wasn't an option either.

Option three, he could go to a different location and pray facing a different direction so people would not notice.

But years before, Solomon had asked God for something. In I Kings 8 he said: *Lord, when your people disobey you and end up as captives in a foreign land, give them a chance for mercy. If they repent, **and if they pray towards Jerusalem**, hear their prayer, Lord.*

For seventy years Daniel had been doing just that. For seventy years he had been opening his window, setting his face towards Jerusalem, and praying three times a day to the God of Heaven. And God had honored him for that. God showed him the mercy that Solomon asked for. Lots of other people had been killed, but Daniel and his friends had not only lived but had been consistently elevated to positions of authority.

As Daniel had prayed like this, God had never one time let him down, and Daniel was determined to keep praying. He prayed in the same place, at the same times, in the same way, facing the same direction as he always had. You just have to love people who do right and never change!

So Daniel did what he always did. He flung open his windows, and with 122 sets of eyes down below watching and waiting, Daniel fell to his knees and entered into the Holy of Holies in Heaven, where he met with God one more wonderful time.

A Deceitful Concern

Daniel 6:12 *Then they came near, and spake before the king concerning the king's decree; Hast thou not signed a decree, that every man that shall ask a petition of any God or man within thirty days, save of thee, O king, shall be cast into the den of lions? The king answered and said, The thing is true, according to the law of the Medes and Persians, which altereth not.* **13** *Then answered they and said before the king, That Daniel, which is of the children of the captivity of Judah, regardeth not thee, O king, nor the decree that thou hast signed, but maketh his petition three times a day.*

Can you not just hear the mock concern dripping off of their forked tongues? O King, haven't you signed a decree that no one can ask anything of anyone but you for thirty days. O dear, we don't quite know how to say this, it just kills us to have to bring this to your attention, but Daniel...

And as soon as they got to the word Daniel, King Darius realized his mistake. This was the best advisor, the best friend any king could ever have, and Darius had just signed his death warrant.

A Desperate Search

Daniel 6:14 *Then the king, when he heard these words, was sore displeased with himself...*

I love what an old commentator named Adam Clark said here:

> And well he might (be), when through his excessive folly he passed a law that, for its ostensible object, would have been a disgrace most to an idiot.

Clark was right. This was a stupid law that even an idiot could have seen through if he had thought about it for even a moment. But the damage was done; the law was signed.

Daniel 6:14 *Then the king, when he heard these words, was sore displeased with himself, and set his heart on Daniel to deliver him: and he laboured till the going down of the sun to deliver him.*

Darius thought a lot of Daniel. This man could have, no doubt, found another advisor, but he knew what he had in Daniel. So he looked all day for the one thing he needed most – a loophole, some way to save Daniel's life.

In studying this passage, I am struck by the fact that in all of it, the only person looking for a loophole was the king. The wicked advisors did not want a loophole; they loved their wicked plan. Daniel did not want a loophole; he would rather die than find a way not to pray. The king was the only one looking for a way out. We'll come back to that thought in just a bit.

106

A Dramatic Night

Daniel 6:15 *Then these men assembled unto the king, and said unto the king, Know, O king, that the law of the Medes and Persians is, That no decree nor statute which the king establisheth may be changed.*

At sunset, 122 smirking advisors showed up before the king. They condescendingly reminded him that his law was non-revocable, and he may as well quit looking for a loophole.

Daniel 6:16 *Then the king commanded, and they brought Daniel, and cast him into the den of lions. Now the king spake and said unto Daniel, Thy God whom thou servest continually, he will deliver thee.*

It seems like every time he turns around, Daniel is hearing a deadly knock on the door. As a teenager, Arioch knocks on the door, and when Daniel opens it he is there with the ax ready to cut off Daniel's head. Through the years, one king's dream after another brought the knock on Daniel's door. Now, as an old man, the knock comes one more time. I wonder what Daniel was thinking as he left his room behind, maybe for the last time?

Looking at the order of events in the verse, you find that Daniel was thrown into the lions den, followed by the king crying out, "Daniel, Thy God whom thou servest continually, he will deliver thee!" I do not know if Darius really believed it. I do not even know if Daniel expected it. But I do know that there was a bunch of hungry lions waiting for Daniel at the bottom of that cavern.

Daniel 6:17 *And a stone was brought, and laid upon the mouth of the den; and the king sealed it with his own signet, and with the signet of his lords; that the purpose might not be changed concerning Daniel.*

Look at the exact words of the verse and an awesome picture develops. Daniel is cast into the den of lions. Ancient animal dens like that were huge caverns divided into multiple chambers. In order to clean part of it, meat would be dropped into one part, and when the animals came for it a gate from above was closed behind them. Some of these dens could hold hundreds of hungry animals, and they were used for just this purpose. They had open grates above them so the gruesome sight could be seen by all, and an opening at one side so the victims could be thrown in. After Daniel is cast in, a stone is laid over the mouth of the cavern so there can be no escape. Then a man with a blob of hot wax comes by and drops it onto the stone. While it is still hot, Darius the king walks over and presses his signet into it. Then the lords come over, those other two presidents, and they press their signets into it. Those marks on the stone would ensure that no one dared to open up the den and rescue Daniel or their own lives would be forfeit.

Can you imagine the mixed reactions? Darius walks away mad at himself, mad at his advisors, scared for Daniel. The conspirators practically skip away, pumping their fists; they have gotten their man. And then there is Daniel. The old man hits the bottom of the cavern, regains his composure, looks up, and sees a bunch of 400-pound, hungry, man-eating cats licking their chops.

Daniel 6:18 *Then the king went to his palace, and passed the night fasting: neither were instruments of musick brought before him: and his sleep went from him.* **19** *Then the king arose very early in the morning, and went in haste unto the den of lions.*

Darius is torn up. He does not eat that night, he chases the musicians out, and he does not sleep a wink all night. And then at the crack of dawn, he bolts out of bed and heads for the den of lions.

Daniel 6:20 *And when he came to the den, he cried with a lamentable voice unto Daniel: and the king spake and said to Daniel, O Daniel, servant of the living God, is thy God, whom thou servest continually, able to deliver thee from the lions?*

The king is crying; we see that in the word *lamentable*. He says, "O Daniel, has that God that you always served delivered you? Daniel, I can't make you out, are you still there? Are you still alive?"

Daniel 6:21 *Then said Daniel unto the king, O king, live for ever.*

Do you ever wonder if people in the Bible had a little bit of mischief to them? I wonder if, when Darius called out, Daniel waited a few seconds... before he answered. Daniel said, *O King, live forever!* "Hey king, dry your eyes, I'm alive!"

Daniel 6:22 *My God hath sent his angel, and hath shut the lions' mouths, that they have not hurt me: forasmuch as before him innocency was found in me; and also before thee, O king, have I done no hurt.*

Daniel did not just let Darius know he was alive, he also told him why. God sent an angel and shut the lions' mouths. I love this. I can just imagine God giving out angelic assignments for the day in Heaven:

"Ok, Gabriel, take a message for me to some of my servants in Jerusalem. Guilo, there is a kid near Samaria that needs some encouragement. Michael, go down to Babylon for me. I need you to go into the lions' den. Daniel is in there because he prayed to Me. Go smack those lions around a little bit and make sure they keep their teeth off of my servant. I love that old man, let's keep him alive a while longer."

Daniel 6:23 *Then was the king exceeding glad for him, and commanded that they should take Daniel up out of the den. So Daniel was taken up out of the den, and no manner of hurt was found upon him, because he believed in his God.*

Happy ending! But as in the words of great $19.95 advertisers throughout the years, "But wait, there's more..."

A Deadly Mistake

Have you ever missed something that was so obvious, that when you realized you missed it you just wanted to kick yourself? We built the steeple that was on top of our old church building. We built it right there in the back room. One problem: when we got it done, we realized that it was too wide at the base to fit through the door! We never even considered that! We had to remove the entire door frame to get it out.

109

That may sound like a really dumb oversight, but it is not nearly as dumb as the oversight these so-called wise men had in their plan:

Daniel 6:24 *And the king commanded, and they brought those men which had accused Daniel, and they cast them into the den of lions, them, their children, and their wives; and the lions had the mastery of them, and brake all their bones in pieces or ever they came at the bottom of the den.*

They spent all of their time trying to find a way to kill Daniel, but they never gave a second's thought to keeping themselves alive! Had they written their own safety into the decree, they could not have been touched, but they did not. That is slam-your-head-in-a-car-door kind of dumb. Do you know what this proves, though? It proves that no one stuffed those lions with food to keep Daniel alive. Those lions were starved, mostly because an angel refused to let them eat all night. These men caused their own deaths and the death of their families when they came after the man of God. This was one deadly mistake.

Daniel 6:25 *Then king Darius wrote unto all people, nations, and languages, that dwell in all the earth; Peace be multiplied unto you.* **26** *I make a decree, That in every dominion of my kingdom men tremble and fear before the God of Daniel: for he is the living God, and stedfast for ever, and his kingdom that which shall not be destroyed, and his dominion shall be even unto the end.* **27** *He delivereth and rescueth, and he worketh signs and wonders in heaven and in earth, who hath delivered Daniel from the power of the lions.* **28** *So this Daniel prospered in the reign of Darius, and in the reign of Cyrus the Persian.*

Once more a heathen king puts into writing a testimony to the greatness of the one true God. This was much the same sentiment that Nebuchadnezzar conveyed many years earlier, and it is the same type of awe of God that every human should still be showing today.

110

Chapter 9
Terror from the Deep

Daniel 7:1 *In the first year of Belshazzar king of Babylon Daniel had a dream and visions of his head upon his bed: then he wrote the dream, and told the sum of the matters.* **2** *Daniel spake and said, I saw in my vision by night, and, behold, the four winds of the heaven strove upon the great sea.* **3** *And four great beasts came up from the sea, diverse one from another.* **4** *The first was like a lion, and had eagle's wings: I beheld till the wings thereof were plucked, and it was lifted up from the earth, and made stand upon the feet as a man, and a man's heart was given to it.* **5** *And behold another beast, a second, like to a bear, and it raised up itself on one side, and it had three ribs in the mouth of it between the teeth of it: and they said thus unto it, Arise, devour much flesh.* **6** *After this I beheld, and lo another, like a leopard, which had upon the back of it four wings of a fowl; the beast had also four heads; and dominion was given to it.* **7** *After this I saw in the night visions, and behold a fourth beast, dreadful and terrible, and strong exceedingly; and it had great iron teeth: it devoured and brake in pieces, and stamped the residue with the feet of it: and it was diverse from all the beasts that were before it; and it had ten horns.* **8** *I considered the horns, and, behold, there came up among them another little horn, before whom there were three of the first horns plucked up by the roots: and, behold, in* *this horn were eyes like the eyes of man, and a mouth speaking great things.* **9** *I beheld till the thrones were cast down, and the Ancient of days did sit, whose garment was white as snow, and the hair of his head like the pure wool: his throne was like the fiery flame, and his wheels as burning fire.* **10** *A fiery stream issued and came forth from before him: thousand thousands ministered unto him, and ten thousand times ten thousand stood before him: the judgment was set, and the books were opened.* **11** *I beheld then because of the voice of the great words which the horn spake: I beheld even till the beast was slain, and his body destroyed, and given to the burning flame.* **12** *As concerning the rest of the beasts, they had their dominion taken away: yet their lives were prolonged for a season and time.* **13** *I saw in the night visions, and, behold, one like the Son of man came with the clouds of heaven, and came to the Ancient of days, and they brought him near before him.* **14** *And there was given him dominion, and glory, and a kingdom, that all people, nations, and languages, should serve him: his dominion is an everlasting dominion, which shall not pass away, and his kingdom that which shall not be destroyed.* **15** *I Daniel was grieved in my spirit in the midst of my body, and the visions of my head troubled me.* **16** *I came near unto one of them that stood by, and asked him the truth of all this. So he told me, and made me know the interpretation of the things.* **17** *These great beasts, which are four, are four kings, which shall arise out of the earth.* **18** *But the saints of the most High shall take the kingdom, and possess the kingdom for ever, even for ever and ever.* **19** *Then I would know the truth of the fourth beast, which was diverse from all the others, exceeding dreadful, whose teeth were of iron, and his nails of brass; which devoured, brake in pieces, and stamped the residue with his feet;* **20** *And of the ten horns that were in his head, and of the other which came up, and before whom three fell; even of that horn that had eyes, and a mouth that spake very great things, whose look was more stout than his fellows.* **21** *I beheld, and the same horn made war with the saints, and prevailed against them;* **22** *Until the Ancient of days came, and judgment*

112

was given to the saints of the most High; and the time came that the saints possessed the kingdom. **23** *Thus he said, The fourth beast shall be the fourth kingdom upon earth, which shall be diverse from all kingdoms, and shall devour the whole earth, and shall tread it down, and break it in pieces.* **24** *And the ten horns out of this kingdom are ten kings that shall arise: and another shall rise after them; and he shall be diverse from the first, and he shall subdue three kings.* **25** *And he shall speak great words against the most High, and shall wear out the saints of the most High, and think to change times and laws: and they shall be given into his hand until a time and times and the dividing of time.* **26** *But the judgment shall sit, and they shall take away his dominion, to consume and to destroy it unto the end.* **27** *And the kingdom and dominion, and the greatness of the kingdom under the whole heaven, shall be given to the people of the saints of the most High, whose kingdom is an everlasting kingdom, and all dominions shall serve and obey him.* **28** *Hitherto is the end of the matter. As for me Daniel, my cogitations much troubled me, and my countenance changed in me: but I kept the matter in my heart.*

Six chapters of Daniel are behind us. They have truly been *Breathtaking.* They have also been chronological. What you see in those first six chapters happened in order, one thing after another. Those first six chapters dealt a whole lot with the day to day events happening during the seventy year captivity and in the personal lives of Daniel, Shadrach, Meshach, and Abednego.

All of that changes during the last half of this book. The last king we saw in Daniel 6 was Cyrus the Persian, who reigned after Darius the Mede. But as Daniel 7 begins, Daniel is recounting events that happened back during the first year of the reign of Belshazzar. Chapter eight jumps to the third year of Belshazzar. Chapter nine goes to the first year of Darius. Chapter ten goes to the third year of Cyrus. Chapter eleven and twelve go back to the first year of Darius. And where much of the first six chapters dealt with the here and now of

Daniel's day, all of the last six chapters deal with visions that God gave Daniel of things yet to come.

These last six chapters are some of the most attacked chapters in the Bible. Liberals and Bible deniers hate them because they so accurately tell of events that happened hundreds of years after Daniel died. Those liberals and Bible deniers try to "post-date" them, claiming that they were written after the events happened! The trouble with that is, there is not one shred of evidence for it! On the contrary, historians from that very era and the few generations to follow, including the great Josephus, universally testified that Daniel wrote all of this book in his lifetime. And the events that he prophesied included vivid descriptions of the Roman Empire during the time of Christ and beyond, by which time Daniel had been dead for hundreds and hundreds of years. Yet the entire book of Daniel was already into the settled Jewish Cannon of the Old Testament. So anyone that tries to tell you that Daniel was written after Daniel's lifetime is quite simply lying.

Throughout the first six chapters, other people have been having terrifying dreams, and Daniel has been called upon to interpret them. Other people have sat straight up in bed gasping for air. Other people have awakened drenched with sweat and with pounding hearts. But in Daniel 7, Daniel opens his own personal diary and tells us about the time that the nightmare was for him.

A Gathering Storm

Daniel 7:1 *In the first year of Belshazzar king of Babylon Daniel had a dream and visions of his head upon his bed: then he wrote the dream, and told the sum of the matters. 2 Daniel spake and said, I saw in my vision by night, and, behold, the four winds of the heaven strove upon the great sea.*

Daniel was way up in his eighties. Belshazzar was on the throne, and unbeknownst to most, the Chaldean Empire was in its last days. As Daniel put his old head down on his pillow one night, it is doubtful that he knew just how troubled of a night he was going to have. Sometime during that night the old man began to toss and turn. He was twitching and writhing, as an awful nightmare unfolded before him.

In his dream Daniel was looking out at a great sea. The scene was not at all peaceful. There was a huge storm brewing. Many storms are caused by the wind clashing from two different directions, but in this case, winds from all four directions are converging on and clashing over this great sea. Clouds are dark and thick. The sound is deafening. To Daniel, he was right there on that beach, in the midst of that howling, screaming cyclone. His throat was tightening as he saw waves of incredible size forming and crashing towards him. Pitch black night, heavy atmosphere, no let up in the storm's intensity, no certainty as to which direction of wind will prevail. This storm was the worst hurricane you could ever imagine times 100. And things were about to get much, much worse.

A Ghostly Specter

Daniel 7:3 *And four great beasts came up from the sea, diverse one from another.*

The first part of Daniel's dream was a huge, general sort of horror. It was a huge ocean, whipped up by a huge storm. But the second part of his dream got a lot more focused. While he was watching this huge storm on this troubled sea, he saw something that just was not normal. The water seemed to boil up like a huge mountain, because some *thing* was coming up out of it. A giant beast rose up out of this troubled sea. And then another, then another, then another.

Daniel would find out just a bit later what all of this meant. But I want to let you in on part of it now. If you remember what the book of the Revelation says, you know what this great sea is. In the Bible, the sea is often used as a picture of the world of humanity, the nations:

Revelation 17:15 *And he saith unto me, The waters which thou sawest, where the whore sitteth, are peoples, and multitudes, and nations, and tongues.*

115

This sea, whipped about by a storm of epic proportions, is the world of men, the nations of the world. From that troubled sea Daniel saw four beasts arise. Look down at verse seventeen, and let's get a quick preview of what these beasts represent:

Daniel 7:17 *These great beasts, which are four, are four kings, which shall arise out of the earth.*

So the sea is mankind, and the four beasts are kings, which are synonymous with their kingdoms. Do you remember Nebuchadnezzar's dream of a huge image? How many kingdoms were there? Four. The Babylonians, the Medo-Persians, the Grecians, and the Romans, who then re-appeared as the revived Roman Empire of the last days. These beasts of Daniel 7 are going to correspond with the image of Daniel 2, only with much greater and much more frightening detail.

Daniel 7:4 *The first was like a lion, and had eagle's wings: I beheld till the wings thereof were plucked, and it was lifted up from the earth, and made stand upon the feet as a man, and a man's heart was given to it.*

This first beast is the Babylonian Empire, the Chaldeans. It is described here as being like a lion with eagle's wings. In Jeremiah 4:7 and Isaiah 5:29, Babylon is described as a lion. In Jeremiah 48:40 and Ezekiel 17:3 and 7, it is described as flying like an eagle. The imagery fits. But it gets even more exact. The wings of the eagle were plucked, and the beast was lifted up from the earth and made to stand up on its feet like a man, and a man's heart was given to it. This might sound familiar to you:

Daniel 4:33 *The same hour was the thing fulfilled upon Nebuchadnezzar: and he was driven from men, and did eat grass as oxen, and his body was wet with the dew of heaven, till his hairs were grown like eagles' feathers, and his nails like birds' claws.* **34** *And at the end of the days I Nebuchadnezzar lifted up mine eyes unto heaven, and mine understanding returned unto me...*

116

The mighty Nebuchadnezzar, who had always acted like a beast, was reduced to a beast. For seven years his hair grew like eagle's feathers, and he crawled around on all fours. At the end of that time, he was given back his sense, his human heart, and he stood up again like a man. The hair/feathers were clipped away. This was the end of his time as a beast, but it was also very near to the end of the beastly kingdom of Babylon. Just a few short years later it would fall, a victim to the second ghostly specter to rise up out of the troubled sea.

Daniel 7:5 *And behold another beast, a second, like to a bear, and it raised up itself on one side, and it had three ribs in the mouth of it between the teeth of it: and they said thus unto it, Arise, devour much flesh.*

This second beast coincides with the second part of Nebuchadnezzar's image, the silver torso and arms of the Medes and the Persians. This time, the Medo-Persian Empire is described as a bear. The image fits. The lion was an appropriate symbol for Babylon, the king of beasts to represent the greatest of kingdoms. The bear was likewise an appropriate symbol for Medo-Persia. The bear is a huge, lumbering animal that wins battles by sheer size and force. There is no "subtlety" to a bear; there is no "finesse" in how it handles things. The Medes and Persians were just like that.

Many nations sent out their soldiers in small sections, so that they would not risk losing everything at once. Britain did that during WWII during the Battle of Britain over the English Channel. They would often send up seven or eight Spitfires to face off against 150 German Messershmidts. The Medes and Persians did not do that. In every battle, they committed overwhelming numbers to the fight. It was all or nothing for them. What they could not accomplish by strategy they did by sheer volume. They just kept coming and coming and coming by the thousands till they overwhelmed their enemies.

Notice that this bear is described as raising itself up on one side. One side was stronger than the other, raising up for the attack. The Persian side of the empire was stronger than the Median side. There was one king from the Median side, Darius. From that point on all the kings were Persian, and the empire simply became known as Persia. It was known as Persia till 1935, when it officially became known as Iran. The Persian Empire, though destroyed down to a fraction of what it once was, still exists more than two millennia after Daniel's day.

This bear that Daniel saw in his dream, while poised to attack, was also still eating the remnants of its last victim. There were three bloody ribs in the mouth of this bear. As if that was not startling enough for this dear old man, as he watched, the ribs in the mouth of the bear started talking to the bear. Daniel heard them say *Arise, devour much flesh.* Again, this fits perfectly. When the Medes and Persians started to gain in power, three countries formed an alliance against them. Babylon, Egypt, and Lydia banded together to stand against them. They had no hope of surviving. By the time Medo-Persia was done with that animal, all that was left were three ribs that were so totally subjugated that they were in the mouth of the bear saying, "Go ahead, eat all you like, we can't stop you."

But this second massive beast, so huge and powerful, was itself going to fall prey to the third ghostly specter to rise up from the waters.

Daniel 7:6 *After this I beheld, and lo another, like a leopard, which had upon the back of it four wings of a fowl; the beast had also four heads; and dominion was given to it.*

This third beast coincides with the third part of the image in Nebuchadnezzar's dream, the belly and thighs of brass, the Grecian Empire. This third beast that Daniel saw was like a leopard. Smaller than the lion, smaller than the bear, but far more cunning than either of them. It did not have two wings, it had four. When you get a leopard with four wings, what you have is one fast cat! But this leopard that was given dominion over the bear was also a freak: it had four heads.

The Grecian Empire under Alexander the Great was not initially as big or strong as Babylon or Medo-Persia had been.

118

But what they were was very fast and very clever. Their military tactics are still in textbooks. They used maneuverability to keep their opponent in the wrong spot, facing the wrong way while they destroyed them from the side or from behind. By the time he was thirty-two years old Alexander had conquered the world. But keep this in mind: at the time Daniel wrote down this dream, he could not have known of Greece or Alexander. What he also could not have known was that Alexander would die young, and his kingdom would be split into four parts, with each of his four generals becoming the head over one part. If the kingdom had split three ways, Daniel's vision would have been wrong. If it had split five ways, Daniel's vision would have been wrong. If it had split two or six or seven ways, or if it had never split at all, if it had done anything but split exactly four ways Daniel's vision would have been wrong. But Daniel's vision was not wrong. It was dead on the money, just like everything else in the Bible.

Daniel 7:7 *After this I saw in the night visions, and behold a fourth beast, dreadful and terrible, and strong exceedingly; and it had great iron teeth: it devoured and brake in pieces, and stamped the residue with the feet of it: and it was diverse from all the beasts that were before it; and it had ten horns.*

This fourth beast coincides with the fourth part of the image in Nebuchadnezzar's dream, the legs of iron that transitioned into feet of iron mixed with clay. Daniel was seeing the Roman Empire in this last beast to come up out of the water. As Daniel saw this last beast, his bad dream became a full-fledged nightmare. Notice that in all of the first three descriptions of beasts that Daniel gave, he simply described what they were. A lion with eagle's wings. A bear with three ribs in its mouth. A leopard with four wings and four heads. Think about parts of speech, then look at verse seven again and notice what is different:

Dreadful... terrible... strong *exceedingly...* **great** *iron teeth.*

Daniel never used a single adjective to describe the first three beasts. But when he got to this last beast, it was one adjective after another, and none of them were good. This last beast shook Daniel up. And did you notice that he did not say that it was "like" something? The first kingdom was *like* a lion, the second was *like* a bear, the third was *like* a leopard. This fourth beast was not *like* anything that Daniel had ever seen or known. It was a vague, dark, furious, unstoppable demon with great iron teeth.

When Rome came onto the scene, it did just what Daniel describes here. It broke and devoured and stomped every other nation on the world scene. By a century before Christ it was the beast of the world. This beast that Daniel could not describe as being like anything else did have one definite characteristic other than its great iron teeth. It had ten horns. Horns in the Bible are a symbol for kingdoms or divisions of kingdoms or alliances that form kingdoms. This corresponds to the ten toes of the image in Nebuchadnezzar's dream, partly made of iron, partly of clay. This part of the beast has not come into existence yet. It is the revived Roman Empire.

Daniel saw these horns on this unspeakable beast. But in this dream, things kept going from bad to worse to awful. As he looked at those horns, look what he saw and heard:

Daniel 7:8 *I considered the horns, and, behold, there came up among them another little horn, before whom there were three of the first horns plucked up by the roots: and, behold, in this horn were eyes like the eyes of man, and a mouth speaking great things.*

As Daniel was considering these horns on this awful beast, another horn sprang up right in the middle of them. When it did, it took out three of the first ten horns. There is a war going on right on the top of the head of this beast between some of the horns on its head! That horn that sprung up was not as big and prominent as the first ten had been. It is called a "little horn." It has "self-esteem issues." It is determined to prove that it is something big, so it goes to war and conquers three other horns.

As Daniel is watching all of this, his amazement turns to abject horror when he notices that the little horn on that beast's head has eyes, man's eyes. It also has a mouth, and it is "speaking great things." That Hebrew phrase means it is boasting and bragging. So Daniel is now looking at a beast that is not like anything else, something that is *dreadful, terrible, strong, great,* with iron teeth and ten horns. It grows another horn in front of him, that horn plucks up three of the first horns by the roots leaving a bloody open wound, and then the little horn meets eyes with Daniel and begins bragging and boasting while the beast lumbers up out of the surf onto the beach.

A Glorious Sovereign

Daniel 7:9 *I beheld till the thrones were cast down, and the Ancient of days did sit, whose garment was white as snow, and the hair of his head like the pure wool: his throne was like the fiery flame, and his wheels as burning fire.* **10** *A fiery stream issued and came forth from before him: thousand thousands ministered unto him, and ten thousand times ten thousand stood before him: the judgment was set, and the books were opened.*

By now you should be going back and forth in your mind between Daniel's dream here in chapter seven and Nebuchadnezzar's dream in chapter two and putting things together. If you are, then you have probably figured out by now that this next part of Daniel's dream corresponds to the stone in Nebuchadnezzar's dream that crushed the entire image and filled the entire earth.

Daniel saw God. Three times in this chapter God is referred to by a name that is used nowhere else in the Bible, *The Ancient of Days.* That name carries so much meaning. It means that He is eternal. He is now what He has always been, there has never been a time when He was not, and there has never been a time when He was different from what He is now.

121

He has all the wisdom of eternity, and He has always been just exactly as wise as He is now. Time has added nothing to Him, nor has it taken anything away from Him. He is the Ancient of Days. When He arrived on the scene, Daniel saw all these earthly thrones cast down. The kingdoms of the lion and the bear and the leopard and the beast were all swept away. Daniel, this blessed old man, was able to give us the only human-type description of God the Father in the entire Bible.[5] He said:

...whose garment was white as snow, and the hair of his head like the pure wool: his throne was like the fiery flame, and his wheels as burning fire. **10** *A fiery stream issued and came forth from before him*

He is dressed all in snow-white clothing. His hair is white as pure wool. His throne looks like it is made out of pure flame. Like all oriental thrones it moves on wheels, but even the wheels of His throne look like they are made of fire as well. And this picture of fire gets even more amazing when Daniel realizes that not only is the fire not hurting this great God on the throne, but He Himself is producing fire and sending it out ahead of Him like a heavenly blow torch. All of the sudden, those four beasts do not sound so impressive anymore! It is amazing how unimpressive the greatest of mankind can be when God gets on the scene.

Daniel 7:10 *A fiery stream issued and came forth from before him: thousand thousands ministered unto him, and ten thousand times ten thousand stood before him: the judgment was set, and the books were opened.*

The four beasts are seen by themselves, no one in attendance. But when Daniel sees the Ancient of Days, His court is filled with servants, millions of them. It is judgment day, and everyone is gathered to hear the verdict that God will render as the books are opened.

Daniel 7:11 *I beheld then because of the voice of the great words which the horn spake...*

After seeing the Ancient of Days, it is almost easy to forget about that, isn't it! There was this horn, this little horn, this annoying yet dangerous little pipsqueak that had been running its mouth. Whatever it had said, it was bad enough that God had noticed and had opened a session of His court to deal with it.

Daniel 7:11 *I beheld then because of the voice of the great words which the horn spake: I beheld even till the beast was slain, and his body destroyed, and given to the burning flame.*

That should sound oh, so familiar:

Revelation 19:20 *And the beast was taken, and with him the false prophet that wrought miracles before him, with which he deceived them that had received the mark of the beast, and them that worshipped his image. These both were cast alive into a lake of fire burning with brimstone.*

This little horn of the beast is none other than the Antichrist of the book of the Revelation. Remember that. Little horn is Antichrist. He will boast... he will brag... and he will burn...

Daniel 7:12 *As concerning the rest of the beasts, they had their dominion taken away: yet their lives were prolonged for a season and time.*

When the Tribulation Period comes, remnants of the first three beasts will be on earth, allied against God. And when the Antichrist, the little horn of the great beast is defeated, he will go straight to Hell forever, yet the remnants of those other kingdoms will continue to live on through the Millennial Reign of Christ. Their dominion will be gone, they will have no power, but they will still exist.

And there is a definite period for which they will exist. The Bible calls it here a *season and time*.

A season can be different things in the Bible. It can be a "little season" like you see in Revelation 6:11 and Revelation 20:3, or it can be a great season lasting for centuries. In this case, the season is one thousand years, the Millennial Reign of Christ that Revelation 20 tells us about. A *time* in the Bible means a year. These kingdoms will exist after the little horn is destroyed for 1001 more years, the one thousand years of peace

123

whether they like it or not, and the one year after Satan is loosed from the bottomless pit. In that last year Satan will whip them up into a frenzy for one more battle against God, and when God defeats them that time, they will be destroyed and gone forever.

But the dream is not over just yet.

Daniel 7:13 *I saw in the night visions, and, behold, one like the Son of man came with the clouds of heaven, and came to the Ancient of days, and they brought him near before him.* **14** *And there was given him dominion, and glory, and a kingdom, that all people, nations, and languages, should serve him: his dominion is an everlasting dominion, which shall not pass away, and his kingdom that which shall not be destroyed.*

Daniel saw the storm, and the beasts, and the Ancient of Days, and the last battle. And then he saw Jesus, the Son of Man, coming before His Father with the clouds of Heaven. He is conducted up to the throne, and God the Father gives Him, God the Son, the ruling dominion of all the universe forever. The rest of Scripture testifies to that very fact:

Psalm 110:1 *The LORD said unto my Lord, Sit thou at my right hand, until I make thine enemies thy footstool.*

The Father is saying: *Just sit here on my right hand Jesus, till I give you all of this to rule over...*

That exact same thing is repeated in Matthew 22, Mark 12, Luke 20, Hebrews 1, and Hebrews 10. God the Father is going to commit everything to the Son; His kingdom will be an everlasting kingdom and will never be destroyed.

A Grieved Spirit

After seeing how the dream ended, it is almost surprising that these are the next words we come to:

Daniel 7:15 *I Daniel was grieved in my spirit in the midst of my body, and the visions of my head troubled me.*

Daniel's heart was troubled, his body literally hurt from it, and his mind was a mess. Daniel was more perceptive than we are, and he picked up on some things from the dream that will be explained in the rest of this chapter.

Daniel 7:16 *I came near unto one of them that stood by, and asked him the truth of all this. So he told me, and made me know the interpretation of the things.*

Every time Daniel had a vision there was an angel standing somewhere nearby. Daniel went to one of those angels and said, "I have to know..." So the angel began to tell him.

Daniel 7:17 *These great beasts, which are four, are four kings, which shall arise out of the earth.*

This we already know; Babylon, Medo-Persia, Greece, Rome.

Daniel 7:18 *But the saints of the most High shall take the kingdom, and possess the kingdom for ever, even for ever and ever.*

By his answer, this angel let us know a little bit about what concern was on Daniel's heart. He was concerned for the people of God, us. How would we fare in all this? The angel told him that the saints of the Most High would take the kingdom and possess it forever and ever. But isn't Christ the one that is given the kingdom according to verses thirteen and fourteen? Yes, but look at another passage:

Romans 8:16 *The Spirit itself beareth witness with our spirit, that we are the children of God:* **17** *And if children, then heirs; heirs of God, and **joint-heirs with Christ**; if so be that we suffer with him, that we may be also glorified together.*

What is His is ours! If we suffer with Him, we will be glorified with Him. When He takes the kingdom, we take the kingdom. The people of God will be all right. But even with that good news, Daniel is still troubled, and there are still some things he has to know.

Daniel 7:19 *Then I would know the truth of the fourth beast, which was diverse from all the others, exceeding dreadful, whose teeth were of iron, and his nails of brass; which devoured, brake in pieces, and stamped the residue with his feet;* **20** *And of the ten horns that were in his head, and of the other which came up, and before whom three fell; even of*

125

that horn that had eyes, and a mouth that spake very great things, whose look was more stout than his fellows.

Daniel described the beast to the angel exactly the way we read about it, except for the fact that the little horn is now described as *more stout than his fellows.* In other words, he may have been little, but he was more powerful than they were. Daniel is focused in on this one little horn on this one big beast. And the next verse tells us why and lets us know why Daniel is still so upset even after seeing a vision of God and His coming kingdom.

Daniel 7:21 *I beheld, and the same horn made war with the saints, and prevailed against them;* **22** *Until the Ancient of days came, and judgment was given to the saints of the most High; and the time came that the saints possessed the kingdom.*

Daniel is telling the angel what he saw so that the angel can tell him what it means. We are just now in the text finding out about this part of Daniel's nightmare. After Daniel saw this beast and the talking horn and before He saw God and His coming kingdom, he saw this little horn make war with the saints and win. This horn that started his conquest by plucking up three of his allies soon turns his attention to the people of God. That troubled Daniel; he knew that bad times were ahead for us.

Daniel 7:23 *Thus he* **(the angel)** *said, The fourth beast shall be the fourth kingdom upon earth, which shall be diverse from all kingdoms, and shall devour the whole earth, and shall tread it down, and break it in pieces.* **(the Old Roman Empire)** **24** *And the ten horns out of this kingdom are ten kings that shall arise* **(The Revived Roman Empire)***: and another shall rise after them* **(the Antichrist)***; and he shall be diverse from the first, and he shall subdue three kings.* **25** *And he shall speak great words against the most High, and shall wear out the saints of the most High, and think to change times and laws: and they shall be given into his hand until a time and times and the dividing of time.*

For a time, times, and half a time, a total of three and a half years, Antichrist will seem to be unstoppable. This is the

126

last half of the Tribulation Period, what Jeremiah 30:7 calls *the time of Jacob's trouble.* He will try to change the world; all the laws, even the way time is measured. For seven years he will be on the scene. The first three and a half years will be bad; the last three and a half years will be awful. But look what comes next:

Daniel 7:26 *But the judgment shall sit* **(that time we already saw when the Ancient of Days holds court)**, *and they shall take away his* **(Antichirist's)** *dominion, to consume and to destroy it unto the end.* **27** *And the kingdom and dominion, and the greatness of the kingdom under the whole heaven, shall be given to the people of the saints of the most High, whose kingdom is an everlasting kingdom, and all dominions shall serve and obey him.*

Terror came from the deep. There was a Gathering Storm, a Ghostly Specter, a Glorious Sovereign, yet Daniel still had a Grieved Spirit. He said:

Daniel 7:28 *Hitherto is the end of the matter. As for me Daniel, my cogitations* **(thoughts)** *much troubled me, and my countenance changed in me: but I kept the matter in my heart.*

Even after seeing how well things turned out, Daniel still woke up badly troubled by the dream. And the part that troubled him was what the saints were going to go through before things all turned out well. Before Jesus puts the devil and the Antichrist down forever, things are going to get very, very hard here on earth for the people of God. Because of that, there are two things you desperately need. One, you need to spend every day of your life walking very close to God. Two, Christians, you need each other!

Chapter 10

Broken Hearts, Broken Horns

Daniel 8:1 *In the third year of the reign of king Belshazzar a vision appeared unto me, even unto me Daniel, after that which appeared unto me at the first.* **2** *And I saw in a vision; and it came to pass, when I saw, that I was at Shushan in the palace, which is in the province of Elam; and I saw in a vision, and I was by the river of Ulai.* **3** *Then I lifted up mine eyes, and saw, and, behold, there stood before the river a ram which had two horns: and the two horns were high; but one was higher than the other, and the higher came up last.* **4** *I saw the ram pushing westward, and northward, and southward; so that no beasts might stand before him, neither was there any that could deliver out of his hand; but he did according to his will, and became great.* **5** *And as I was considering, behold, an he goat came from the west on the face of the whole earth, and touched not the ground: and the goat had a notable horn between his eyes.* **6** *And he came to the ram that had two horns, which I had seen standing before the river, and ran unto him in the fury of his power.* **7** *And I saw him come close unto the ram, and he was moved with choler against him, and smote the ram, and brake his two horns: and there was no power in the ram to stand before him, but he cast him down to the ground,* *and stamped upon him: and there was none that could deliver the ram out of his hand.* **8** *Therefore the he goat waxed very great: and when he was strong, the great horn was broken; and for it came up four notable ones toward the four winds of heaven.* **9** *And out of one of them came forth a little horn, which waxed exceeding great, toward the south, and toward the east, and toward the pleasant land.* **10** *And it waxed great, even to the host of heaven; and it cast down some of the host and of the stars to the ground, and stamped upon them.* **11** *Yea, he magnified himself even to the prince of the host, and by him the daily sacrifice was taken away, and the place of his sanctuary was cast down.* **12** *And an host was given him against the daily sacrifice by reason of transgression, and it cast down the truth to the ground; and it practised, and prospered.* **13** *Then I heard one saint speaking, and another saint said unto that certain saint which spake, How long shall be the vision concerning the daily sacrifice, and the transgression of desolation, to give both the sanctuary and the host to be trodden under foot?* **14** *And he said unto me, Unto two thousand and three hundred days; then shall the sanctuary be cleansed.* **15** *And it came to pass, when I, even I Daniel, had seen the vision, and sought for the meaning, then, behold, there stood before me as the appearance of a man.* **16** *And I heard a man's voice between the banks of Ulai, which called, and said, Gabriel, make this man to understand the vision.* **17** *So he came near where I stood: and when he came, I was afraid, and fell upon my face: but he said unto me, Understand, O son of man: for at the time of the end shall be the vision.* **18** *Now as he was speaking with me, I was in a deep sleep on my face toward the ground: but he touched me, and set me upright.* **19** *And he said, Behold, I will make thee know what shall be in the last end of the indignation: for at the time appointed the end shall be.* **20** *The ram which thou sawest having two horns are the kings of Media and Persia.* **21** *And the rough goat is the king of Grecia: and the great horn that is between his eyes is the first king.* **22** *Now that being broken, whereas four stood up for it, four kingdoms shall stand up out of the nation, but not in his power.*

23 *And in the latter time of their kingdom, when the transgressors are come to the full, a king of fierce countenance, and understanding dark sentences, shall stand up.* **24** *And his power shall be mighty, but not by his own power: and he shall destroy wonderfully, and shall prosper, and practise, and shall destroy the mighty and the holy people.* **25** *And through his policy also he shall cause craft to prosper in his hand; and he shall magnify himself in his heart, and by peace shall destroy many: he shall also stand up against the Prince of princes; but he shall be broken without hand.* **26** *And the vision of the evening and the morning which was told is true: wherefore shut thou up the vision; for it shall be for many days.* **27** *And I Daniel fainted, and was sick certain days; afterward I rose up, and did the king's business; and I was astonished at the vision, but none understood it.*

We've been going verse by verse through Daniel, and it has indeed been *Breathtaking*. The first six chapters dealt with day to day events in the lives of Daniel, Shadrach, Meshach, Abednego, and the kings that they served under. But as we saw in the last chapter, everything changed as of chapter seven. Daniel began in that chapter to tell us of several different dreams and visions that God gave him, all of which dealt with prophetical things to come. In chapter seven Daniel saw himself looking out at a great sea, and he saw four monstrous beasts come up out of it. That vision terrified him beyond measure, even after he saw the Ancient of Days make everything right. Chapter eight is going to bring another vision, Daniel is going to be torn up inside all over again, and we are going to be amazed at how accurate God's Word is once more.

A Battle by the River

You may remember that in Daniel 2:4, the Book of Daniel went from using the Hebrew language to using the Chaldean's language of Syriac. That was the language of the Gentiles. That makes perfect sense since chapters two through four dealt primarily with Gentile world powers, and the

Chaldeans were heavily written of both in history and in prophecy until Daniel 7:28. But as of chapter eight, Daniel will change back to the Hebrew language. That is God's way of letting us know that from here till the end of the book, things will heavily concern the Jewish people.

Daniel 8:1 *In the third year of the reign of king Belshazzar a vision appeared unto me, even unto me Daniel, after that which appeared unto me at the first.* **2** *And I saw in a vision; and it came to pass, when I saw, that I was at Shushan in the palace, which is in the province of Elam; and I saw in a vision, and I was by the river of Ulai.*

It was the third year of Belshazzar's reign, which would make it 538 B.C. Daniel was physically in Babylon, but in a vision he saw himself in Shushan. Shushan was at that time the capital of the Medo-Persian Empire. It was about 250 miles due east from Babylon. Both Nehemiah and Esther lived in Shushan. Shushan had much cooler weather than Babylon, and it was common for the royal family of Persia to live in Shushan during the summer and move to Babylon during the winters. In his vision Daniel saw that he was by the river Ulai. That river was a small river that was formed by two streams that passed on either side of Shushan. Historians tell us that the water from that river was cool and clean and had an excellent taste. When the Persians went out into battle, many of the nobles would carry some of that water with them to battle. So the scene that Daniel saw was a beautiful, refreshing scene. But that beauty was about to give way to a battle.

Daniel 8:3 *Then I lifted up mine eyes, and saw, and, behold, there stood before the river a ram which had two horns: and the two horns were high; but one was higher than the other, and the higher came up last.*

This is a verse that is not hard at all to understand, especially since Daniel got an angelic explanation of it towards the end of the chapter:

Daniel 8:20 *The ram which thou sawest having two horns are the kings of Media and Persia.*

Having gone this far in the book of Daniel, we also know exactly what verse three means when it says that one horn was higher than the other, and the higher horn came up last. The Persian side of the empire became by far the stronger side, even though the Mede side of the empire was first. We saw that typified another way by the bear in chapter seven that was raising up on one side. This was something Daniel would become personally familiar with; he would live through it when the Medes and the Persians defeated Babylon.

Daniel 8:4 *I saw the ram pushing westward, and northward, and southward; so that no beasts might stand before him, neither was there any that could deliver out of his hand; but he did according to his will, and became great.*

This verse perfectly describes the movements and conquests of the Medo-Persian Empire. They went westward and conquered Babylon, Mesopotamia, Syria, and Asia Minor. They moved southward and conquered Judea, Egypt, Ethiopia, Libya and India. They moved northward and conquered Colchis, Armenia, Iberia, and the dwellers on the Caspian Sea.[6]

The Medes and the Persians at that time were unstoppable. Just like the verse says, *he did according to his will, and became great.* But any kingdom or nation that expects that kind of dominance to last forever is going to end up with a broken heart, and broken horns.

Daniel 8:5 *And as I was considering, behold, an he goat came from the west on the face of the whole earth, and touched not the ground: and the goat had a notable horn between his eyes.*

Just like the first part of the vision, this is easy to decipher since it is point blank explained later in the chapter:

Daniel 8:21 *And the rough goat is the king of Grecia: and the great horn that is between his eyes is the first king.*

That rough goat was the king of Grecia in general. But that goat had a big bad horn between his eyes, and that was none other than Alexander the Great. Greece was west of Persia, as verse five says. When Alexander started moving east to take on the Medo-Persians, he moved so quickly that verse

133

five says he *touched not the ground.* In a day when there was no such thing as an airplane, much less an air force, Alexander used soldiers on foot and conquered the world in six years time. His biggest rival was the then current world superpower, the Medes and Persians. And that is where Daniel began to see the battle by the river:

Daniel 8:6 *And he came to the ram that had two horns, which I had seen standing before the river, and ran unto him in the fury of his power. 7 And I saw him come close unto the ram, and he was moved with choler against him, and smote the ram, and brake his two horns: and there was no power in the ram to stand before him, but he cast him down to the ground, and stamped upon him: and there was none that could deliver the ram out of his hand.*

There are two important words to notice in these verses: fury in verse six and choler, which means *bitter rage,* in verse seven. Most of these world conquests were not personal; it was just nation versus nation, and may the best army win. But with Alexander this was intensely personal. History records Alexander as a man that did not like to be challenged. He felt like everyone should do what he said, the very moment he said it, and give him whatever he wanted, the moment he wanted it. But there was an enemy general that had no intentions of bowing to the "upstart" Alexander. Darius Codomannus was the Emperor of Persia and commander of the armies. He intended to stop Alexander in his tracks, and he tried it three times. Each time, as was the normal way of the Persians, he committed huge numbers of soldiers to the field, dwarfing what Alexander had to work with. Alexander didn't take that as a normal part of battle; he took it as a personal insult. He literally got enraged at the thought of it.

Let me tell you how remarkable the rise of Alexander the Great was. He had an army of about 30,000 men and 5,000 horses. He was fighting against a Medo-Persian army estimated to be nearly a million strong. He was facing overwhelming odds in manpower. Three times these two armies met, three times Alexander and Darius Codomannus matched leadership skills. Now please remember that at the time Daniel was given this vision, Greece was a little group of people called "The Goat People." They were no threat at all. It was the Medo-Persians who were about to be in charge of the world. That is what makes this prophecy of Daniel so remarkable. When he predicted that Greece would defeat Persia, that would be like me today predicting that Grover, NC, would defeat the Chinese army one day. Again, this is why Bible deniers try to post date the book of Daniel and claim that someone else wrote it hundreds of years after Daniel, after these events had already happened. But here is what they will not tell you, the great historian Josephus records that Alexander himself read the prophecies of Daniel and clearly recognized himself in them. Because of that, he dealt kindly with the Jews since Daniel was a Jew.

But surprising or not, Daniel's vision was right. In all three battles, fought at Granicus, Issus, and Arbela, the tiny army of Alexander routed the massive army of the Persians. In the last battle alone the Grecians wiped out some 600,000 soldiers of the Persians.[7] That crippled them and ruined them as a world power. That battle determined the history of the Middle East for the next two hundred years.

A Broken Horn

Daniel 8:8 *Therefore the he goat waxed very great: and when he was strong, the great horn was broken; and for it came up four notable ones toward the four winds of heaven.*

Anyone who has studied any history at all can almost fill in the major blanks here. At thirty-three years old, at the height of his power, as the conqueror of the world, Alexander was called out into eternity to meet with the God he never knew. What you may not know is how it happened. Alexander decided to have a drinking contest with some of his men. After consuming several quarts of liquor, he fell into a drunken stupor, got pneumonia, and died shortly thereafter. Just another great life ruined by booze.

135

Notice that verse eight says when the great horn, Alexander, was broken, four notable ones came up in its place facing towards the four winds of heaven. That is again a perfect prophetical prediction of what later happened. After Alexander died, his empire was split into four parts with each of his generals taking one part. Cassander got Macedonia and Greece; Lysimachus got Asia Minor; Seleucus got Syria and Babylonia; and Ptolemy got Egypt and North Africa.

In his twenties, Alexander sat down and wept, broken hearted because there were no more worlds to conquer. After his broken heart, he became a broken horn, cut off, dead too early, another example of the fact that all human power is a temporary thing.

A Beast Rising

Daniel 8:9 *And out of one of them came forth a little horn, which waxed exceeding great, toward the south, and toward the east, and toward the pleasant land.*

I hope that you remember what we saw in Daniel 7, little horn is Antichrist. That was true then, and it is true now. Sort of...

Let me use another passage of Scripture to explain what I mean.

Ezekiel 28:12 *Son of man, take up a lamentation upon the king of Tyrus, and say unto him, Thus saith the Lord GOD; Thou sealest up the sum, full of wisdom, and perfect in beauty.*

What smart, good looking man is being spoken of here? The King of Tyrus (Tyre). He was a king alive in the days of Ezekiel. Read on:

Ezekiel 28:13 *Thou hast been in Eden the garden of God;*

When is the last time in the Bible Eden was shown to actually exist? Way back in Genesis, before the flood! Was the king of Tyre there? No. Read on:

every precious stone was thy covering, the sardius, topaz, and the diamond, the beryl, the onyx, and the jasper, the sapphire, the emerald, and the carbuncle, and gold: the workmanship of thy tabrets and of thy pipes was prepared in thee in the day that thou wast created. **14** *Thou art the anointed cherub that covereth;*

Was the king of Tyre a Cherubim? No. Read on:

...and I have set thee so: thou wast upon the holy mountain of God; thou hast walked up and down in the midst of the stones of fire. **15** *Thou wast perfect in thy ways from the day that thou wast created, till iniquity was found in thee.* **16** *By the multitude of thy merchandise they have filled the midst of thee with violence, and thou hast sinned: therefore I will cast thee as profane out of the mountain of God: and I will destroy thee, O covering cherub, from the midst of the stones of fire.* **17** *Thine heart was lifted up because of thy beauty, thou hast corrupted thy wisdom by reason of thy brightness: I will cast thee to the ground, I will lay thee before kings, that they may behold thee.*

The anointed Cherub, present in the Garden of Eden, walked up and down in the midst of the stones of fire, went up against God, and God laid him low. Who is being talked about in this passage? Satan? I thought it was the King of Tyre! The King of Tyre? I thought it was Satan! It was both. The King of Tyre was a little example of a bigger problem; he was a type of Satan, he was a good picture of the devil. This often happens in Scripture, where one thing or one person serves as a type of another. The King of Tyre was as close a human facsimile of the devil as he could be. And this is exactly what you will see in Daniel 8:9-25. Little Horn is Antichrist to come, and he is also a man named Antiochus who has already come, a few hundred years after the days of Daniel. Let's look at this.

According to verse nine this little horn waxed exceeding great toward the south and the east and towards "the pleasant land." After Seleucus died, a man from that line named Antiochus Epiphanes came to power over Syria. He was a brutal, bloodthirsty, cold-hearted killer. Many of the great kings before him had been just like that; Nebuchadnezzar, Cyrus, etc. But here is the difference: unlike them, Antiochus held a special hatred in his heart for what

137

verse nine calls "The Pleasant Land." According to Psalm 106:24 that is a name for Israel, Judea. Antiochus hated the Jews, Judaism, and all Israel with an unbelievably bitter hatred.

Daniel 8:10 *And it* **(the little horn,)** *waxed great, even to the host of heaven; and it cast down some of the host and of the stars to the ground, and stamped upon them.* **11** *Yea, he magnified himself even to the prince of the host, and by him the daily sacrifice was taken away, and the place of his sanctuary was cast down.* **12** *And an host was given him against the daily sacrifice by reason of transgression, and it cast down the truth to the ground; and it practised, and prospered.*

At this point in the text pretty much every part of it has a double reference. We can see in each phrase something that Antiochus did that points to something that Antichrist will do even worse. Look at each phrase. We are told that this little horn waxed (grew) great "even to the host of heaven, and it cast down some of the host and of the stars to the ground." Antiochus Epiphanes fulfilled that in type. He tortured and killed many of the priests and officials of the Temple of God, including the priest Eleazar and seven others when they refused to eat swine's flesh. Antichrist will fulfill this in reality. He and the rest of the satanic trinity will cause a literal war in Heaven that we read about in Revelation 12. He will lose but not without doing a lot of damage first.

We are also told that the little horn magnifies himself even unto the prince of the host. Antiochus fulfilled that in type on December 15, 168 B.C. On that day, he stood against God in the vilest way he could think of. He entered the Temple and sacrificed an enormous sow on the altar. Then he forced the priest to swallow its flesh and sprinkled the blood all over the Temple. Then he carried a large idol of Jupiter into the Holy of Holies and set it up as god. By the way, this would never have been possible if God's people had not forsaken Him and gone their own way without Him. When His people were right with him, anyone but the high priest that walked into that Most Holy Place would have died instantly. You lose a lot when you go your own way instead of God's way. But as for what was done in type by Antiochus, Antichrist will fulfill it in reality when he enters the rebuilt Temple in Jerusalem during the Tribulation Period. II Thessalonians 2:4 tells us that at that time, Antichrist will come into that new Temple and proclaim himself as god.

We also find that the little horn takes away the daily sacrifice and casts down the sanctuary. Antiochus did this in reality. He stopped the daily sacrifice, by which the people and God kept in contact with each other each day. The sanctuary was, at that point, cast down. It was useless and degraded. Antichrist will do it in reality as well. The sanctuary will again be, at that point, cast down. It will be useless and degraded.

Then we find that the little horn is given a "host" (an army to enforce his will) against the daily sacrifice because of the transgression of the people. Antiochus fulfilled this, he enforced his wishes by the sword. Antichrist will do the very same during the Tribulation Period.

We are also told that the little horn casts down truth to the ground, practices and prospers. In other words, lies are his way of life, yet it works out very well for him as far as immediate results are concerned. Antiochus fulfilled that perfectly. History records him as being the worst of liars. Antichrist will be just like that:

2 Thessalonians 2:9 *Even him, whose coming is after the working of Satan with all power and signs and lying wonders,* **10** *And with all deceivableness of unrighteousness in them that perish; because they received not the love of the truth, that they might be saved.*

There was a liar then, there is a liar to come.

Daniel 8:13 *Then I heard one saint speaking, and another saint said unto that certain saint which spake, How long shall be the vision concerning the daily sacrifice, and the transgression of desolation, to give both the sanctuary and the host to be trodden under foot?* **14** *And he said unto me, Unto two thousand and three hundred days; then shall the sanctuary be cleansed.*

139

These two verses mark one of the greatest prophecies in the Bible. They once again prove beyond a doubt that the Bible is the inspired Word of God. Daniel heard some saints talking in his vision. He has been hearing from angels, but now he is hearing from believers, saints in Glory. One of them has a question, and the other one has already been given word by God as to what the answer is. The first saint asked in Daniel's hearing, "How long will this last? How long will Antiochus get by with this?" The other one answers, "For 2,300 days."

Now see this. On September 6, 171 B.C., Antiochus started his campaign against the Jews and against the Temple. All throughout Palestine altars were set up to Jupiter, and everyone was commanded to worship them. But in a little town called Modin, seventeen miles northwest of Jerusalem, there was an old Jewish priest named Matthias who had five grown sons. Not only would Matthias not bow to this abomination, he killed the ambassador of Antiochus, and he and his sons started a rebellion. One of his boys was named Judas the Macabee. That name Macabee means "The Hammer." Judas the Hammer was appropriately named. He became one of the main leaders of the rebellion. Would you like to hear about an early Christmas gift? On December 25, 165 B.C., the Hammer and his forces recaptured, cleansed, and re-dedicated the Temple of God. And do you know what is significant about that date? It was exactly 2,300 days from September 6, 171 B.C., when Antiochus began his campaign of evil. Daniel prophesied exactly to the day how long this would last, and he was right. The Bible was right. There is no book on earth like the Bible![8]

Daniel 8:15 *And it came to pass, when I, even I Daniel, had seen the vision, and sought for the meaning, then, behold, there stood before me as the appearance of a man.* **16** *And I heard a man's voice between the banks of Ulai, which called, and said, Gabriel, make this man to understand the vision.* **17** *So he came near where I stood: and when he came, I was afraid, and fell upon my face: but he said unto me, Understand, O son of man: for at the time of the end shall be the vision.*

These verses will let you know something remarkable about the prophets and their prophecies. They were given these prophecies by God, but many times they themselves had no clue what they meant! Daniel did not know what all of this was about, so he was searching his heart and mind for the meaning. That is when he heard a voice from between the banks of the Ulai River, meaning that the voice came from an angel who was in the river, or on the river, or over the river itself. The voice called out to Gabriel and told Gabriel to explain to Daniel about the vision. Gabriel made his way to Daniel, and Daniel fell on his face, terrified. Gabriel then began to unfold to Daniel the truth of the vision, and he started with the fact that this vision was *for the time of the end.*

Antiochus was not at *the time of the end.* Antiochus was more than 2,100 years ago. This lets us know again that even though Antiochus fulfilled all of this in type, the ultimate fulfillment will come during the Tribulation Period, in the person of the antichrist.

Daniel 8:18 *Now as he was speaking with me, I was in a deep sleep on my face toward the ground: but he touched me, and set me upright.* **19** *And he said, Behold, I will make thee know what shall be in the last end of the indignation: for at the time appointed the end shall be.* **20** *The ram which thou sawest having two horns are the kings of Media and Persia.* **21** *And the rough goat is the king of Grecia: and the great horn that is between his eyes is the first king.* **22** *Now that being broken, whereas four stood up for it, four kingdoms shall stand up out of the nation, but not in his power.*

All of this we already know and have already covered. But notice that verse nineteen speaks of what will be in *the last end of the indignation.* What Antiochus did was "the indignation." What Antichrist will do will be "the last end of the indignation."

Daniel 8:23 *And in the latter time of their kingdom, when the transgressors are come to the full, a king of fierce countenance, and understanding dark sentences, shall stand up.*

141

It was at the latter end of the power of the Grecian Empire that Antiochus arose. Antiochus was a *king of fierce countenance*, but Antichrist will be much more so. Antiochus *understood dark sentences*, meaning that he was shrewd and wise even though it was all used for evil. Again, Antichrist will be just like that only much worse.

Daniel 8:24 *And his power shall be mighty, but not by his own power: and he shall destroy wonderfully, and shall prosper, and practise, and shall destroy the mighty and the holy people.*

Antiochus was powerful, but he was powerful because Satan was empowering him and driving him. Oh, how much worse things will be the second time around. Antichrist will be so satanically empowered that he will make Antiochus look like Mary Poppins. Antiochus destroyed, Antichrist will *destroy wonderfully* Antiochus killed tens of thousands of Jews, Antichrist will kill millions.

Daniel 8:25a *And through his policy* **(his evilly prudent decisions)** *also he shall cause craft* **(deceit)** *to prosper in his hand; and he shall magnify himself in his heart, and by peace shall destroy many:*

Antiochus was a devious politician, and deceit flourished in his reign. Antichrist will be Antiochus times ten to the power of five when it comes to deceit. He will convince the entire world to sign onto the peace treaty to end all peace treaties, even getting Jews and Arabs to both go along with it. Then halfway into the treaty period, he will break that treaty. His "peaceful" beginning will lure everyone into going along with him, and then he will turn out to be the greatest mass murderer in history.

You know what I would not want to be? I would not want to be someone who does not accept Christ as his Savior and finds himself in the Tribulation Period facing the Antichrist. I would especially not want to find myself as a Jew who does not accept Christ as his Savior and finds himself in the Tribulation Period facing the Antichrist, knowing how bad he hates them.

Another Broken Horn

Daniel 8:25b *...he shall also stand up against the Prince of princes; but he shall be broken without hand. 26 And the vision of the evening and the morning which was told is true: wherefore shut thou up the vision; for it shall be for many days. 27 And I Daniel fainted, and was sick certain days; afterward I rose up, and did the king's business; and I was astonished at the vision, but none understood it.*

Thank God for what you read in verse twenty-five. Antichrist will be broken without hand. It will not be a military coup that undoes him. He will challenge the Prince of Princes, the Lord Jesus Christ, and he will lose royally. No surprise there; anyone who ever goes up against Jesus loses.

This vision, God told Daniel to "shut it up." Daniel never did try to explain all of it. God gave Daniel a sealed vision, and then he unsealed it for us when He gave us the book of the Revelation.

As this chapter draws to a close, I am amazed again by the fact that for a second time, Daniel sees a vision in which God wins and evil loses, yet Daniel is scared and sickened by what he sees. That lets us know just how very bad things were under Antiochus, and how much worse things will be during the Tribulation Period. Antiochus operated for around seven years. Antichrist will operate for some seven years. One was and the other will be a liar. One was and the other will be a mass murderer. One tried and the other will try to defeat God Himself.

But here is a key difference: in the days of Antiochus, people could read the Word of God, see what was going on, and accept God. During the days of Antichrist, according to II Thessalonians 2:11-12, God will not allow that. If you do not accept Christ now while He is drawing you and the Rapture takes place, the Christians are gone, the Tribulation Period begins, and Antichrist comes to power, God will send you a strong delusion. You will believe the lie of Antichrist, and you will not get saved. I know that there are popular books that tell you that people will reject God, then see the Rapture and the

143

Tribulation Period, and then choose to get saved. But the Bible says otherwise. You *can* accept Jesus now, or you *will* accept Antichrist then. And if you do, you will be just one more person who ends up with a broken heart, as a broken horn, tortured on earth, and then burning in Hell. You need to accept Jesus now, while you can. You have seen how accurate the Bible is. I just showed you the fulfilled prophecy of the 2,300 days. You have no reason to doubt the Bible and no reason to reject the Lord Jesus.

Chapter 11

The Pinnacle of Prophecy

Daniel 9:1 *In the first year of Darius the son of Ahasuerus, of the seed of the Medes, which was made king over the realm of the Chaldeans;* **2** *In the first year of his reign I Daniel understood by books the number of the years, whereof the word of the LORD came to Jeremiah the prophet, that he would accomplish seventy years in the desolations of Jerusalem.* **3** *And I set my face unto the Lord God, to seek by prayer and supplications, with fasting, and sackcloth, and ashes:* **4** *And I prayed unto the LORD my God, and made my confession, and said, O Lord, the great and dreadful God, keeping the covenant and mercy to them that love him, and to them that keep his commandments;* **5** *We have sinned, and have committed iniquity, and have done wickedly, and have rebelled, even by departing from thy precepts and from thy judgments:* **6** *Neither have we hearkened unto thy servants the prophets, which spake in thy name to our kings, our princes, and our fathers, and to all the people of the land.* **7** *O Lord, righteousness belongeth unto thee, but unto us confusion of faces, as at this day; to the men of Judah, and to the inhabitants of Jerusalem, and unto all Israel, that are near, and that are far off, through all the countries whither thou hast driven them,* *because of their trespass that they have trespassed against thee.* **8** *O Lord, to us belongeth confusion of face, to our kings, to our princes, and to our fathers, because we have sinned against thee.* **9** *To the Lord our God belong mercies and forgivenesses, though we have rebelled against him;* **10** *Neither have we obeyed the voice of the LORD our God, to walk in his laws, which he set before us by his servants the prophets.* **11** *Yea, all Israel have transgressed thy law, even by departing, that they might not obey thy voice; therefore the curse is poured upon us, and the oath that is written in the law of Moses the servant of God, because we have sinned against him.* **12** *And he hath confirmed his words, which he spake against us, and against our judges that judged us, by bringing upon us a great evil: for under the whole heaven hath not been done as hath been done upon Jerusalem.* **13** *As it is written in the law of Moses, all this evil is come upon us: yet made we not our prayer before the LORD our God, that we might turn from our iniquities, and understand thy truth.* **14** *Therefore hath the LORD watched upon the evil, and brought it upon us: for the LORD our God is righteous in all his works which he doeth: for we obeyed not his voice.* **15** *And now, O Lord our God, that hast brought thy people forth out of the land of Egypt with a mighty hand, and hast gotten thee renown, as at this day; we have sinned, we have done wickedly.* **16** *O Lord, according to all thy righteousness, I beseech thee, let thine anger and thy fury be turned away from thy city Jerusalem, thy holy mountain: because for our sins, and for the iniquities of our fathers, Jerusalem and thy people are become a reproach to all that are about us.* **17** *Now therefore, O our God, hear the prayer of thy servant, and his supplications, and cause thy face to shine upon thy sanctuary that is desolate, for the Lord's sake.* **18** *O my God, incline thine ear, and hear; open thine eyes, and behold our desolations, and the city which is called by thy name: for we do not present our supplications before thee for our righteousnesses, but for thy great mercies.* **19** *O Lord, hear; O Lord, forgive; O Lord, hearken and do; defer not, for thine own sake, O my God: for thy city and thy people are* *called by thy name.* **20** *And whiles I was speaking, and praying, and confessing my sin and the sin of my people Israel, and presenting my supplication before the LORD my God for the holy mountain of my God;* **21** *Yea, whiles I was speaking in prayer, even the man Gabriel, whom I had seen in the vision at the beginning, being caused to fly swiftly, touched me about the time of the evening oblation.* **22** *And he informed me, and talked with me, and said, O Daniel, I am now come forth to give thee skill and understanding.* **23** *At the beginning of thy supplications the commandment came forth, and I am come to shew thee; for thou art greatly beloved: therefore understand the matter, and consider the vision.* **24** *Seventy weeks are determined upon thy people and upon thy holy city, to finish the transgression, and to make an end of sins, and to make reconciliation for iniquity, and to bring in everlasting righteousness, and to seal up the vision and prophecy, and to anoint the most Holy.* **25** *Know therefore and understand, that from the going forth of the commandment to restore and to build Jerusalem unto the Messiah the Prince shall be seven weeks, and threescore and two weeks: the street shall be built again, and the wall, even in troublous times.* **26** *And after threescore and two weeks shall Messiah be cut off, but not for himself: and the people of the prince that shall come shall destroy the city and the sanctuary; and the end thereof shall be with a flood, and unto the end of the war desolations are determined.* **27** *And he shall confirm the covenant with many for one week: and in the midst of the week he shall cause the sacrifice and the oblation to cease, and for the overspreading of abominations he shall make it desolate, even until the consummation, and that determined shall be poured upon the desolate.*

In chapters seven and eight, I know you have been as amazed as I have by the stunning accuracy of the prophecies of Daniel. But as great as the prophecies in those chapters are, the prophecies in Daniel chapter nine are even greater still. H.A. Ironsides called it "the greatest of all time prophecy." Sir

Edward Denny called it "the backbone of prophecy." I have chosen to call it *The Pinnacle Of Prophecy.*

Seventy Years

Daniel 9:1 *In the first year of Darius the son of Ahasuerus, of the seed of the Medes, which was made king over the realm of the Chaldeans; 2 In the first year of his reign I Daniel understood by books the number of the years, whereof the word of the LORD came to Jeremiah the prophet, that he would accomplish seventy years in the desolations of Jerusalem.*

The beginning of this chapter takes us back in time to the first year of Darius the Mede. He was the king who took over at the end of Daniel 5 when the Medo-Persians captured Babylon and killed Belshazzar. That great event, the end of the Chaldean Empire, did something to Daniel. The Jews had been captive all those long years to the Babylonians, and now the Babylonians were gone. Daniel wanted to know what that meant for his people. He could not and would not believe that God would leave them in captivity forever.

So Daniel did what every Bible-believing Christian should do when there is a question about something, he sought out answers from God's Word. We have the completed Scripture, sixty-six books, the very last written revelation of God to man. Daniel had about two-thirds of the Old Testament. Part of it had been written by someone that he knew personally. Before he was taken into captivity, as a young man, he had been there in Jerusalem when Jeremiah the prophet was preaching, warning, and writing. The people had refused to listen to that great old prophet back then, but now Daniel sought out his writings like a starving man searches for food. Somehow, from somewhere, he got ahold of a copy of the book of Jeremiah. It is now and was then a long writing, but that did not matter to Daniel. He knew that somewhere in there was an answer to his question: how long will we be in captivity? Here is the answer that he found:

148

Jeremiah 25:11 *And this whole land shall be a desolation, and an astonishment; and these nations shall serve the king of Babylon seventy years.* **12** *And it shall come to pass, when seventy years are accomplished, that I will punish the king of Babylon, and that nation, saith the LORD, for their iniquity, and the land of the Chaldeans, and will make it perpetual desolations.*

Jeremiah 29:10 *For thus saith the LORD, That after seventy years be accomplished at Babylon I will visit you, and perform my good word toward you, in causing you to return to this place.*

When Daniel read this, let me tell you why his heart had to skip a beat: that very year, while Daniel was reading those very words, was their seventieth year of captivity!

Daniel 9:3 *And I set my face unto the Lord God, to seek by prayer and supplications, with fasting, and sackcloth, and ashes:* **4** *And I prayed unto the LORD my God, and made my confession, and said, O Lord, the great and dreadful God, keeping the covenant and mercy to them that love him, and to them that keep his commandments;* **5** *We have sinned, and have committed iniquity, and have done wickedly, and have rebelled, even by departing from thy precepts and from thy judgments:* **6** *Neither have we hearkened unto thy servants the prophets, which spake in thy name to our kings, our princes, and our fathers, and to all the people of the land.*

I love the response of Daniel. He reads that the years of the captivity are officially done that very year. The first thing he does is put off the royal garments, get on sackcloth and ashes, and pray. And what a prayer! First, he glorified God: *O Lord, the great and dreadful God, keeping the covenant and mercy to them that love him, and to them that keep his commandments...* Then he confessed the sin of the people, and this great, godly, humble old man included himself: *We have sinned, and have committed iniquity, and have done wickedly, and have rebelled, even by departing from thy precepts and from thy judgments: Neither have we hearkened unto thy servants the prophets, which spake in thy name to our kings, our princes, and our fathers, and to all the people of the land.*

Those are two essential ingredients to every good prayer. But Daniel was not done yet. Look at the next three sentences, which take up four verses, and watch for the word "belong" both written out and implied:

Daniel 9:7 *O Lord, righteousness **belongeth** unto thee, but unto us* **(implied belongeth)** *confusion of faces, as at this day; to the men of Judah, and to the inhabitants of Jerusalem, and unto all Israel, that are near, and that are far off, through all the countries whither thou hast driven them, because of their trespass that they have trespassed against thee. 8 O Lord, to us **belongeth** confusion of face, to our kings, to our princes, and to our fathers, because we have sinned against thee. 9 To the Lord our God **belong** mercies and forgivenesses, though we have rebelled against him; 10 Neither have we obeyed the voice of the LORD our God, to walk in his laws, which he set before us by his servants the prophets.*

Daniel had everything in his prayer just right. He understood both the character of God and the character of man. God deserves to be accounted as righteous. Daniel knew that he and we and his people deserved *confusion of faces.* Do you know what that is? It is the look of confusion that a sinner gets on his face when he gets busted. Have you ever seen the media's online predator stings? Some officer will go online and pose as a teenage girl, and a middle-aged, pot-bellied, creepy, online predator will proposition her for sex. The cop then gives Mr. Creepy the address and tells him to show up naked. Mr. Creepy, who is also Mr. Idiot, shows up in all of his flabby, pasty-white glory, and walks right in to where the TV cameras are rolling. And then the reporter, not a teenager, not a girl, dressed in a suit and holding a microphone walks in. That look that Mr. I.M. Creepy gets on his face is "confusion of face." He knows he is so busted, he can not figure out what went wrong, and he knows no matter what excuse he makes, life as he knows it is officially over.

To God belongs righteousness. To man belongs confusion of face. But thank God there is more. Verse nine and ten tell us that even though we have rebelled and disobeyed and disregarded His word, **to God belongs mercy and forgiveness!** Daniel knew the score. He knew that he and his people deserved nothing but judgment. But he also knew that God is much more than just a God of judgment; He is also the God of mercy and forgiveness. That is so good. It was good then; it is good now. It was good for the children of Israel, and it is good for us. Have you ever messed up really bad due to your own sin and rebellion and stupidity? You knew you **deserved** judgment, but you **desired** mercy and forgiveness. And what a sweet peace will sweep over your heart when it comes; when God reaches down from Heaven and removes that weight of judgment, and smiles on you one more time, there is just no feeling like that feeling.

Daniel prayed on:

Daniel 9:11 *Yea, all Israel have transgressed thy law, even by departing, that they might not obey thy voice; therefore the curse is poured upon us, and the oath that is written in the law of Moses the servant of God, because we have sinned against him.*

The first part of this verse was Daniel's way of acknowledging that Israel's disobedience had not been an "accidental thing." They did what they did *that they might not obey.* They meant to disobey. I wish people were in the habit of being that honest today. If people were that honest today, they would just go ahead and admit that they actually meant to do wrong:

People say, "We started living together because neither of us could afford to make it on our own. We never intended to actually sleep together or anything."

If people were honest they would say, "We felt like fornicating, and it was a lot more convenient to fornicate if we shacked up, so we chose to shack up."

Teenagers say, "Mom! Dad! I had no idea it was this late!"

151

If they were honest they would say, "Mom! Dad! I was hoping that you had no idea it was this late!"

Teenagers say, "My friends pressured me into sneaking out, and I am so sorry that I went along with them."

If they were honest they would say, "We planned for weeks how we could all slip out of the house together and the only thing in this world I'm really sorry about is that I got caught and that I'm going to get punished."

People say, "I complain and whine because I've had it so hard in life."

If they were honest they would say, "I complain and whine because I feel like the world revolves around me, and that you and everyone else owe me something."

Oh, for people with the honesty of Daniel! The second part of verse eleven introduces something new to the chapter but old to the Children of Israel; this captivity that came because of their sin was written in curse form hundreds of years earlier by Moses. In fact, Moses wrote about it dozens of times. Here is one instance of it:

Leviticus 26:14 *But if ye will not hearken unto me, and will not do all these commandments; 15 And if ye shall despise my statutes, or if your soul abhor my judgments, so that ye will not do all my commandments, but that ye break my covenant: 16 I also will do this unto you; I will even appoint over you terror, consumption, and the burning ague, that shall consume the eyes, and cause sorrow of heart: and ye shall sow your seed in vain, for your enemies shall eat it. 17 And I will set my face against you, and ye shall be slain before your enemies: they that hate you shall reign over you; and ye shall flee when none pursueth you.*

Moses wrote it, Jeremiah repeated it, Israel ignored it, and their children and children's children paid for it.

Daniel 9:12 *And he hath confirmed his words, which he spake against us, and against our judges that judged us, by bringing upon us a great evil: for under the whole heaven hath not been done as hath been done upon Jerusalem.*

Verse twelve brings two new things for us to notice. First, notice that God spoke His words of judgment against the people, but also against the judges that judged them. The reason for that is that their rulers had been leading the way into wickedness! That is not supposed to happen. A real leader, whether a parent, a pastor, or a president, is supposed to stand against evil even if he or she is standing alone. You who are leading in any way need to remember that.

The second thing to notice is that phrase: *for under the whole heaven hath not been done as hath been done upon Jerusalem.* Jerusalem was blessed above all, therefore when she did wrong she was blistered above all. To whom much is given, much is required.

Daniel 9:13 *As it is written in the law of Moses, all this evil is come upon us: yet made we not our prayer before the LORD our God, that we might turn from our iniquities, and understand thy truth.* **14** *Therefore hath the LORD watched upon the evil, and brought it upon us: for the LORD our God is righteous in all his works which he doeth: for we obeyed not his voice.*

There is a great truth taught in these verses. When God brings judgment into our lives, it is supposed to make us recognize and admit that we have disobeyed Him and then repent and make things right. Judah was too stubborn for that. And so they ended up pushing beyond God's last bit of patience with them and paid the price for the next seventy years.

Daniel 9:15 *And now, O Lord our God, that hast brought thy people forth out of the land of Egypt with a mighty hand, and hast gotten thee renown, as at this day; we have sinned, we have done wickedly.*

If you ever want to know how significant the Exodus was, just pay attention to how many times it was mentioned hundreds of years later. Daniel reminded God of it (not implying that God had forgotten) in his prayer, mostly for this reason: God's great name was closely tied to the fate of His people. Even though His people had sinned, the lost world still

153

looked at Israel to get some idea of how great Israel's God was. That is still the case today. Everything you do will, in the eyes of the world, either reflect positively or negatively on God Himself. Live right every day!

Daniel 9:16 *O Lord, according to all thy righteousness, I beseech thee, let thine anger and thy fury be turned away from thy city Jerusalem, thy holy mountain: because for our sins, and for the iniquities of our fathers, Jerusalem and thy people are become a reproach to all that are about us.*

As Daniel continued praying, he said something that will let you know how bad things had gotten for God's people. He said, "Lord, according to thy righteousness turn away your anger and fury, because Jerusalem and your people have become a reproach." In other words, Daniel was saying, "Lord, what we have suffered has been so significant, so severe, that you have fully done your job in punishing us. Lord, we're sorry, please restore us now." He may have gotten that from Jeremiah, who said very much the same thing:

Jeremiah 31:18 *I have surely heard Ephraim bemoaning himself thus; Thou hast chastised me, and I was chastised, as a bullock unaccustomed to the yoke: turn thou me, and I shall be turned; for thou art the LORD my God.*

When God puts the whipping on you, He will not slack off until you are fully whipped, and you ask Him very nicely to please let up.

Daniel 9:17 *Now therefore* **(because of how badly we have been spanked and how sorry we are)**, *O our God, hear the prayer of thy servant, and his supplications, and cause thy face to shine upon thy sanctuary that is desolate, for the Lord's sake.* **18** *O my God, incline thine ear, and hear; open thine eyes, and behold our desolations, and the city which is called by thy name: for we do not present our supplications before thee for our righteousnesses, but for thy great mercies.* **19** *O Lord, hear; O Lord, forgive; O Lord, hearken and do; defer not, for thine own sake, O my God: for thy city and thy people are called by thy name.*

In these verses, Daniel once mentioned the sanctuary, the Temple of God. He twice mentioned Jerusalem, the city of God. He once mentioned the people who were called by the name of God. Daniel asked for mercy for all three; the Temple, the city, and the people. It was mercy that he needed in every place, for every sin.

Seventy years. The sins of the people; idolatry, failure to obey the laws of God, sin upon sin, led to seventy years of captivity in Babylon. But only seventy years. Jeremiah prophesied seventy years, and after seventy years Babylon fell, and the kingdom that was to release them took power. It did not happen after sixty-nine years, it did not happen after seventy-one years. Both the Bible and historians from that very period will tell you that the Babylonian captivity lasted exactly seventy years. Again, the Bible is not like any other book!

Seventy Weeks

Daniel 9:20 *And whiles I was speaking, and praying, and confessing my sin and the sin of my people Israel, and presenting my supplication before the LORD my God for the holy mountain of my God; 21 Yea, whiles I was speaking in prayer, even the man Gabriel, whom I had seen in the vision at the beginning, being caused to fly swiftly, touched me about the time of the evening oblation.*

The "evening oblation" was the sacrifice that, while the Temple stood, had always been offered at 3:00 in the afternoon.[9] The Temple had been in ruins for the better part of seventy years. Daniel had been in captivity for seventy years and had not even seen the spot where the Temple used to be during those long decades. But he was still worshiping God just the same. There is a valuable lesson for the future here. One day we may not be able to meet and worship in our nice new churches or even in old small churches. One day, as it has often been in the past, public worship may be forbidden, and the church may have to go back to meeting secretly in houses or garages or in the woods. If so, worship God just the same!

While Daniel was praying, seeking to understand, Gabriel, who had appeared in the form of a man to Daniel in chapter eight, was sent by God at top speed to bring Daniel an answer. Verse twenty-one says Gabriel was *caused to fly swiftly*. God did not want to keep Daniel waiting. Let me tell you why I think this is: Daniel never kept God waiting, so God did not want to keep Daniel waiting. If you do not want God to keep you waiting, maybe you should not keep Him waiting! The next two verses I believe verify this:

Daniel 9:22 *And he informed me, and talked with me, and said, O Daniel, I am now come forth to give thee skill and understanding.* **23** *At the beginning of thy supplications the commandment came forth, and I am come to shew thee; **for thou art greatly beloved**: therefore understand the matter, and consider the vision.*

God sent this speedy answer based on the fact that Daniel was *greatly beloved* to God. Now think about this: isn't everyone *greatly beloved* of God? In a general sense, yes:

John 3:16 *For God so loved the world, that he gave his only begotten Son, that whosoever believeth in him should not perish, but have everlasting life.*

In the sense that God loved every single person who has ever lived, died for them, and wants to save them, yes, everyone is *greatly beloved* of God. But Daniel was *greatly beloved* in more than just that general way. Daniel had "made himself special" to God. Think of it: as a teenager Daniel was willing to die rather than disappoint God by eating the king's meat. As a young adult he was willing to risk his life by telling the king in so many words that the gods of Babylon that he worshiped were false and worthless gods. Daniel served God his entire lifetime without interruption. He stuck a bony old finger in Belshazzar's face and told him that time was up for him. Then under a new king, as an old man, he went to the lion's den rather than spend a single day not praying. Daniel was not just loved by God in a general sense, he "made himself loveable" to God!

God loves each one of us, but I wonder how many of us are "making ourselves loveable" to God? There is a big difference! But let's get back and see what Gabriel had to say to Daniel.

Daniel 9:24 *Seventy weeks are determined upon thy people and upon thy holy city, to finish the transgression, and to make an end of sins, and to make reconciliation for iniquity, and to bring in everlasting righteousness, and to seal up the vision and prophecy, and to anoint the most Holy.*

Every word and verse of Scripture is inspired and equally inspired. But some verses of Scripture are of such practical and prophetical significance that it is almost as if we are treading on holy ground when we read them. This is one of those verses. Just look at these phrases in it:

Finish the transgression... make an end of sins... make reconciliation for iniquity... bring in everlasting righteousness... anoint the most Holy (with a capital H!)

Even if a person picked up a Bible for the very first time, and it fell open to this verse, just by reading those phrases that person would know it has to describe something unbelievably important! Daniel knew what this meant. When Gabriel got to the part about *anointing the most Holy*, I guarantee you Daniel lost his breath for a moment. *Anointing the most Holy* means that Messiah has arrived. The One that people had been waiting for ever since Genesis 3:15 when God promised that the seed of the woman would bruise the serpent's head, the One that God promised would come through the line of Abraham, and then Jacob, and then Isaac, and then Judah, the One that all of the Old Testament sacrifices pointed to, the Lamb of God that would take away the sins of the world, that "Most Holy One," that Messiah is what Gabriel was talking about. This was the ultimate hope of the Jew, who knew that Messiah would be their King. This was the ultimate hope of every sinner across the world, who knew that they could not get rid of their sin debt without a perfect sacrifice. Believers had been waiting for dozens of generations. Every time a Jewish girl got pregnant she hoped it would be a boy, because

157

she hoped it would be "the Most Holy," the Messiah. And now Daniel is being told that Messiah is coming. He is being told that Messiah will deal with sin and transgression forever and bring in everlasting righteousness. He is being told that Messiah will *seal up the vision and the prophecy.* That is an important phrase. It means that Messiah would complete the revelation of God, so that there would be no more need for visions and prophecies. He did just that when He met with John on the Isle of Patmos and gave him the book of the Revelation, the last Scripture to ever be written. After that, despite what any group or individual says, no more visions or prophecies were ever necessary! Jesus is All in All, and Gabriel told Daniel that He was coming. He also told Daniel when. And the first two words of verse twenty-four are two of the most prophetically significant words in the Bible. Seventy weeks...

Now let's find out about those seventy weeks.

The first thing you need to keep in mind is that Daniel is being given a vision, a prophecy. In all prophecy you will find things that are symbolic, things that represent other things. Remember the four beasts that represented four kingdoms? Remember the little horn that represented Antichrist? Remember the great horn that represented Alexander the great? Remember the great sea that represented mankind? When God speaks prophetically, He normally uses symbolism to do it.

References to time in prophecy also quite often have symbolic meaning. Remember the "time, times, and half a time" of the book of the Revelation? Three and a half years. It is important to remember that references to time can be symbolic, because a week in the Bible can be a literal week, seven days, or it can also represent a period of seven years. Let me show you that.

What was the Sabbath? Saturday, the seventh day, a day of rest. Now look at this:

Leviticus 25:1 *And the LORD spake unto Moses in mount Sinai, saying,* **2** *Speak unto the children of Israel, and say unto them, When ye come into the land which I give you,*

158

then shall the land keep a sabbath unto the LORD. **3 *Six years*** *thou shalt sow thy field* **(you would expect to read "six days")**, *and six years thou shalt prune thy vineyard, and gather in the fruit thereof;* **4** *But in the **seventh year** shall be a sabbath of rest unto the land* **(you would expect to read in the seventh day)**, *a sabbath for the LORD: thou shalt neither sow thy field, nor prune thy vineyard.*

In Exodus 20:9-10, God commanded that man should work seven days and rest one:

Exodus 20:9 *Six days shalt thou labour, and do all thy work:* **10** *But the seventh day is the sabbath of the LORD thy God: in it thou shalt not do any work, thou, nor thy son, nor thy daughter, thy manservant, nor thy maidservant, nor thy cattle, nor thy stranger that is within thy gates:*

But in Leviticus 25, He said, "Work the land for six years. Let it rest the seventh." If you compare Exodus 20 and Leviticus 25, the seven years were just like the seven days. And here is where a little history makes things interesting. According to Jeremiah 34:12-22 and II Chronicles 36:21, the children of Israel disobeyed this command until they built up a seventy year debt of Sabbath years that they had not observed. God had said, "Let the land rest that year, I will make sure that year six is so bountiful that you will not need to sow on year seven." But when the people of Israel saw that great bounty in year six, they thought, "If year six was that good, we can't afford NOT to work in year seven!"

So they disobeyed God till a seventy-year debt of Sabbath years had accumulated. And God in II Chronicles 36:21 said, "I will send you to Babylon for seventy years so that the land can get the rest it deserves!" In order for a seventy-year debt of Sabbaths to accumulate, a 490 year period of disobedience to this command had to build up. In other words, seventy sevens of years.

And that is exactly what the seventy weeks of Daniel 9 are; not seventy cycles of seven days, but seventy cycles of seven years. This will be even easier to see and understand by the time we get to the end of the chapter, so just hang on tight,

159

and believe me for now when I tell you that Gabriel was telling Daniel about a very significant 490 year period that had everything to do with the coming of the Messiah.

Daniel 9:25 *Know therefore and understand, that from the going forth of the commandment to restore and to build Jerusalem unto the Messiah the Prince shall be seven weeks, and threescore and two weeks: the street shall be built again, and the wall, even in troublous times.*

We just read about "seventy weeks." But in this verse, Gabriel mentioned to Daniel a period of "seven weeks, *comma*, and threescore and two weeks." Notice that God could have said "threescore and nine weeks," but He did not. He specifically separated it into one period of seven, and a second period of threescore and two. A "score" is twenty. So if you have seven, and threescore and two, how many weeks do you have? Sixty nine weeks, not seventy. Keep that it mind, it is very important.

We are now dealing with sixty-nine out of these seventy prophetical weeks. If every week is a period of seven years, how long are we talking about? 483 years. Whatever this 483 year period is (and I will show you in a moment what it is) it had a definite beginning point. Gabriel said that the clock on that 483 year period of time would start ticking when the commandment was given to restore and rebuild Jerusalem, which had been leveled seventy years earlier. According to the first two chapters of Nehemiah, this command was given during the twentieth year of King Artaxerxes. The Encyclopedia Britannica talks about that king and that decree, and it sets that date as being March 14, 445 B.C.

Let's start there and look at this.

When Artaxerxes issued the decree to rebuild, the first period of seven weeks began. During that seven-week period (49 years) the last part of Daniel 9:25 literally took place. The street was built again, and the wall, even in troublous times. Read Nehemiah, look at the opposition that the Jews faced, and you find that verse to be dead on. After that, the second period of threescore and two, sixty-two weeks began. Early in the book of Genesis (7:1, 24; 8:3-4) we learn that a Biblical year is not 365 days, but 360 days.[10] Our Gregorian calendar is actually fairly new, and cultures throughout the world used all kinds of different calendars to reckon dates even well up into the twentieth century. So if we figure 69 prophetical weeks, which equals 483 years, we come up with exactly 173,880 days.

Do you remember the 2,300 days we looked at in the last chapter and how impressive of an exact prophecy that was? This will dwarf it. Gabriel told Daniel that from the exact time the commandment was given to rebuild Jerusalem, till the coming of Messiah the Prince, would be 483 Biblical years, exactly 173,880 days. On March 14, 445 B.C. that command was given by Artaxerxes. 173,880 days later, on A.D. April 6, 32, crowds stood by the roadside going into Jerusalem, waving palm branches and shouting "Hosanna! Blessed is He that cometh in the name of the Lord! Hosanna! Blessed is He that cometh in the name of the Lord! Hosanna! Blessed is He that cometh in the name of the Lord!" On that very day, as Jesus rode into Jerusalem on His Triumphal Entry, the Messiah of the Jews presented Himself to the people to accept or reject. Anyone who had read the book of Daniel could have marked their calendar, gotten up that morning and said, "This is it! This is the day that Messiah the Prince will come!" And he would have been right. Please do not get tired of me saying it, the Bible is not like any other book!

After all those years, to the very day, Jesus, Messiah the Prince came. But to the shame of all humanity, the story does not end there:

Daniel 9:26a *And after threescore and two weeks shall Messiah be cut off, but not for himself...*

This prophecy of Daniel made no sense to the Jews. They could not conceive of Messiah being cut off! They should have paid more attention, because much of the Old Testament foretold it:

Isaiah 53:1 *Who hath believed our report? and to whom is the arm of the LORD revealed? 2 For he shall grow* *up before him as a tender plant, and as a root out of a dry ground: he hath no form nor comeliness; and when we shall see him, there is no beauty that we should desire him.* **3** *He is despised and rejected of men; a man of sorrows, and acquainted with grief: and we hid as it were our faces from him; he was despised, and we esteemed him not.* **4** *Surely he hath borne our griefs, and carried our sorrows: yet we did esteem him stricken, smitten of God, and afflicted.* **5** *But he was wounded for our transgressions, he was bruised for our iniquities: the chastisement of our peace was upon him; and with his stripes we are healed.* **6** *All we like sheep have gone astray; we have turned every one to his own way; and the LORD hath laid on him the iniquity of us all.* **7** *He was oppressed, and he was afflicted, yet he opened not his mouth: he is brought as a lamb to the slaughter, and as a sheep before her shearers is dumb, so he openeth not his mouth.* **8** *He was taken from prison and from judgment: and who shall declare his generation? for he was cut off out of the land of the living: for the transgression of my people was he stricken.* **9** *And he made his grave with the wicked, and with the rich in his death; because he had done no violence, neither was any deceit in his mouth.* **10** *Yet it pleased the LORD to bruise him; he hath put him to grief: when thou shalt make his soul an offering for sin, he shall see his seed, he shall prolong his days, and the pleasure of the LORD shall prosper in his hand.* **11** *He shall see of the travail of his soul, and shall be satisfied: by his knowledge shall my righteous servant justify many; for he shall bear their iniquities.* **12** *Therefore will I divide him a portion with the great, and he shall divide the spoil with the strong; because he hath poured out his soul unto death: and he was numbered with the transgressors; and he bare the sin of many, and made intercession for the transgressors.*

Psalm 22:1 *<To the chief Musician upon Aijeleth Shahar, A Psalm of David.> My God, my God, why hast thou forsaken me? why art thou so far from helping me, and from the words of my roaring?*

Psalm 22:17 *I may tell all my bones: they look and stare upon me.* **18** *They part my garments among them, and cast lots upon my vesture.*

Every time a lamb was slain, God was telling the Jews that Messiah would be cut off. When God told Abraham to take Isaac up onto mount Moriah, God was telling the Jews that Messiah would be cut off. Gabriel told Daniel that after Messiah was presented, Messiah would be cut off. But he also specified this: Messiah would be cut off, *but not for Himself:*

Isaiah 53:5 *But he was wounded for our transgressions, he was bruised for our iniquities: the chastisement of our peace was upon him; and with his stripes we are healed.*

Romans 5:8 *But God commendeth his love toward us, in that, while we were yet sinners, Christ died for us.*

Romans 5:6 *For when we were yet without strength, in due time Christ died for the ungodly.*

There has never been a prophecy like this, and there has never been a Savior like this!

Daniel 9:26 *And after threescore and two weeks shall Messiah be cut off, but not for himself: and the people of the prince that shall come shall destroy the city and the sanctuary; and the end thereof shall be with a flood, and unto the end of the war desolations are determined.*

Verse twenty-five called Jesus *Messiah the Prince.* Messiah the Prince came, but the Jews would not have that Man to rule over them. Because they rejected Messiah the Prince, Gabriel prophesied that another prince would come. He prophesied that the people of the prince that will come would destroy the city and the sanctuary. Now watch carefully: when Daniel was receiving this prophecy, he was upset because the city and the sanctuary were that very moment lying in ruins and had been for decades. He had just been told that since the seventy years were up, the commandment from Artaxerxes was about to be issued and all of that was about to be rebuilt. Now he is hearing that his people, the Jews, whose disobedience had caused all of that destruction to begin with,

163

were going to reject their own Messiah, and because of that, the rebuilt city and the rebuilt Temple were going to be demolished all over again. How bad must that have stabbed Daniel's heart? And just like all of the rest of this prophecy, it was dead on. The prince that will come, Antichrist, will be at least partially of Roman descent. And just like verse twenty-six prophesied, his people, the Romans, leveled the city and the Temple. In A.D. 70, nearly forty years after the Jews rejected and crucified Messiah the Prince, Titus and the Roman army obliterated the city and the Temple. That Temple was among the greatest structures on earth of all times, huge marble stones covered in gold. The Romans tore it down stone by stone, set fires up against the rubble, melted the gold off, and left nothing but a heap of ruin. The Jews cried out to Pilate, "Crucify Jesus! Let His blood be on us and on our children!" And God said, "You want it? You got it!" And for 2,000 years the Jews have been haunted and hunted and battered and brutalized by every wicked would-be dictator that has crossed the world scene.

The destruction of Jerusalem in A.D. 70 started a war that still rages to this day, a war in which the devil has been determined to wipe out the Jews, while they still reject their Messiah and refuse His leadership. Verse twenty-six says that the end of this war will be a "flood," which is a prophetical way of describing the flood of hell on earth that falls on Israel in the last days.

Now remember that we are at this point talking about the Antichrist, the evil prince yet to come. But it seems as though we still have some unfinished business, doesn't it? What have we been talking about? The seventy weeks of Daniel. How many weeks have we seen so far? Sixty-nine. 483 years. How many weeks are missing? One, one seven year period is still unaccounted for. Now look at the next verse:

Daniel 9:27 *And he* **(Antichrist, the other prince, the prince that comes because the Jews rejected the real prince)** *shall confirm the covenant with many for one week* **(one seven year period)***: and in the midst of the week* **(after**

164

three and a half years) *he shall cause the sacrifice and the oblation to cease, and for the overspreading of abominations he shall make it desolate, even until the consummation, and that determined shall be poured upon the desolate.*

Ladies and gentlemen, there is your missing week. Daniel's sixty-nine weeks have already come and gone. They started when Artaxerxes commanded to rebuild the Temple, they ended when Jesus rode into Jerusalem and was cut off. At that point, the hands of time on God's prophetic clock stopped. They have been standing still for nearly 2,000 years now, waiting for that seventieth week.

Chapter 12

Of Swords and Sovereigns

Daniel 10:1 *In the third year of Cyrus king of Persia a thing was revealed unto Daniel, whose name was called Belteshazzar; and the thing was true, but the time appointed was long: and he understood the thing, and had understanding of the vision.* **2** *In those days I Daniel was mourning three full weeks.* **3** *I ate no pleasant bread, neither came flesh nor wine in my mouth, neither did I anoint myself at all, till three whole weeks were fulfilled.* **4** *And in the four and twentieth day of the first month, as I was by the side of the great river, which is Hiddekel;* **5** *Then I lifted up mine eyes, and looked, and behold a certain man clothed in linen, whose loins were girded with fine gold of Uphaz:* **6** *His body also was like the beryl, and his face as the appearance of lightning, and his eyes as lamps of fire, and his arms and his feet like in colour to polished brass, and the voice of his words like the voice of a multitude.* **7** *And I Daniel alone saw the vision: for the men that were with me saw not the vision; but a great quaking fell upon them, so that they fled to hide themselves.* **8** *Therefore I was left alone, and saw this great vision, and there remained no strength in me: for my comeliness was turned in me into corruption, and I retained no strength.* **9** *Yet heard I the voice of his words: and* *when I heard the voice of his words, then was I in a deep sleep on my face, and my face toward the ground. 10 And, behold, an hand touched me, which set me upon my knees and upon the palms of my hands. 11 And he said unto me, O Daniel, a man greatly beloved, understand the words that I speak unto thee, and stand upright: for unto thee am I now sent. And when he had spoken this word unto me, I stood trembling. 12 Then said he unto me, Fear not, Daniel: for from the first day that thou didst set thine heart to understand, and to chasten thyself before thy God, thy words were heard, and I am come for thy words. 13 But the prince of the kingdom of Persia withstood me one and twenty days: but, lo, Michael, one of the chief princes, came to help me; and I remained there with the kings of Persia. 14 Now I am come to make thee understand what shall befall thy people in the latter days: for yet the vision is for many days. 15 And when he had spoken such words unto me, I set my face toward the ground, and I became dumb. 16 And, behold, one like the similitude of the sons of men touched my lips: then I opened my mouth, and spake, and said unto him that stood before me, O my lord, by the vision my sorrows are turned upon me, and I have retained no strength. 17 For how can the servant of this my lord talk with this my lord? for as for me, straightway there remained no strength in me, neither is there breath left in me. 18 Then there came again and touched me one like the appearance of a man, and he strengthened me, 19 And said, O man greatly beloved, fear not: peace be unto thee, be strong, yea, be strong. And when he had spoken unto me, I was strengthened, and said, Let my lord speak; for thou hast strengthened me. 20 Then said he, Knowest thou wherefore I come unto thee? and now will I return to fight with the prince of Persia: and when I am gone forth, lo, the prince of Grecia shall come. 21 But I will shew thee that which is noted in the scripture of truth: and there is none that holdeth with me in these things, but Michael your prince.*

Daniel has been every bit as *Breathtaking* as we expected it to be.

But in chapter ten, it takes a twist that will leave you gasping for air if you really get it. So much of the last few chapters have been all about the war that will take place between Antichrist and the Jews during the Tribulation Period. But in Daniel 10, Daniel finds himself caught up in and exposed to something that few people are ever even aware of; Daniel ended up in the middle of a clash of worlds, a battle beyond the three dimensions, a literal warfare between good and evil.

A Broken Ambassador

Daniel 10:1 *In the third year of Cyrus king of Persia a thing was revealed unto Daniel, whose name was called Belteshazzar; and the thing was true, but the time appointed was long: and he understood the thing, and had understanding of the vision.*

Up until this point in the book each chapter has been an individual unit. But when we get to chapter ten, we begin a narrative that will last for the rest of the book. We will cover each chapter individually but understand that they all go together. The conversation that begins between Daniel and the angel begins in chapter ten and does not end till chapter twelve, the very end of the book.

This chapter and event is laid out very differently from those previous to it. In the ones we have seen thus far, a dream or vision was told and then came the explanation. In this one, we find in the very first verse that Daniel knew what the vision was, he knew what it meant, but we are not even going to be told the details of it until the next chapter begins. We do know from this very first verse that what will be told deals with the future, some of which came a few generations after Daniel, some of which is still yet to come even in our day.

Daniel 10:2 *In those days I Daniel was mourning three full weeks. 3 I ate no pleasant bread, neither came flesh nor wine in my mouth, neither did I anoint myself at all, till three whole weeks were fulfilled.*

Daniel has, both politically and spiritually, risen to great prominence. He has, for years, been an ambassador for great men; Nebuchadnezzar, Darius, Cyrus. But he has, above all, been an ambassador for the great God. Daniel has represented the King of Kings with the highest of dignity. But when we look at him in this verse, we see that Daniel is voluntarily broken before God, and again, it is because of his burden for his people.

A Bright Appearing

Daniel 10:4 *And in the four and twentieth day of the first month, as I was by the side of the great river, which is Hiddekel; 5 Then I lifted up mine eyes, and looked, and behold a certain man clothed in linen, whose loins were girded with fine gold of Uphaz: 6 His body also was like the beryl, and his face as the appearance of lightning, and his eyes as lamps of fire, and his arms and his feet like in colour to polished brass, and the voice of his words like the voice of a multitude.*

Daniel was by the Hiddikel, which is another name for the great Tigris River. It was in the month of Nisan, the first month of the Jewish year. In that month, in Exodus 12, God told his people to mourn for seven days, to eat no unleavened bread for seven days, to remember their bondage in Egypt. Daniel, this great old man, is doing three times what God asked. God responds to that kind of devotion. After twenty-one days, Daniel looked up, and there was a man, an angel in the appearance of a man, standing by him. He was awesome in appearance. And let me tell you something about him that we will find out in just a few moments: he was also battle-scarred.

Daniel 10:7 *And I Daniel alone saw the vision: for the men that were with me saw not the vision; but a great quaking fell upon them, so that they fled to hide themselves.*

Daniel was not alone... and then he was alone. Get the details of this: the people that were with Daniel did not see a thing. Yet when that angel arrived, even though the men could not see him, they *felt* something. The verse says a *great*

170

quaking fell upon them. Not on the ground, on them. For no apparent reason they started shaking uncontrollably with fear and bolted! There is power in the unseen world that dwarfs anything we have in the seen world.

Daniel 10:8 *Therefore I was left alone, and saw this great vision, and there remained no strength in me: for my comeliness was turned in me into corruption, and I retained no strength. 9 Yet heard I the voice of his words: and when I heard the voice of his words, then was I in a deep sleep on my face, and my face toward the ground.*

Notice the progression. Daniel was left alone and saw the great vision. He had already seen it, but then the scared little people scurried off, and he could really *SEE IT.* Sometimes, you really can not see a "great vision" while scared people are around! A second thing to notice is this: when Daniel saw what he saw, when he came into the presence of holiness, his comeliness was turned into corruption. In other words, he looked at the best he had to offer and realized he was not some big special thing after all. That being the case, I tend to think that a lot of people have not spent much time in an angel's presence, let alone God's presence.

Daniel 10:9 *Yet heard I the voice of his words: and when I heard the voice of his words, then was I in a deep sleep on my face, and my face toward the ground. 10 And, behold, an hand touched me, which set me upon my knees and upon the palms of my hands.*

I love this. It is not God's desire to knock you down flat on your face, but it is not His desire to *immediately* stand you up nice and tall either. If God can put you in any position He desires, the first position He will put you on is on your hands and knees.

A Battle for the Ages

Daniel 10:11 *And he said unto me, O Daniel, a man greatly beloved, understand the words that I speak unto thee, and stand upright: for unto thee am I now sent. And when he had spoken this word unto me, I stood trembling.*

171

The first thing this angel did was put Daniel in kneeling position. When Daniel gave him no trouble with that, the angel said, "Daniel, God loves you. Stand up." Before God will ever stand you up, He will bow you down.

This angel was sent directly to, and for, Daniel.

Daniel 10:12 *Then said he unto me, Fear not, Daniel: for from the first day that thou didst set thine heart to understand* **(twenty-one days ago)**, *and to chasten thyself before thy God* **(twenty-one days ago)**, *thy words were heard* **(twenty-one days ago)**, *and I am come for thy words* **(and I left twenty-one days ago to get here***).*

Angels are a little faster than that. They do not take twenty-one days to get from Heaven to Earth, they take mere moments to get from Heaven to Earth. So why did it take this one twenty-one days?

Daniel 10:13 *But the prince of the kingdom of Persia withstood me one and twenty days: but, lo, Michael, one of the chief princes, came to help me; and I remained there with the kings of Persia.*

This verse is one of the most stunning verses in the Bible. It peels back the veil of the hidden world and shows us things unseen, yet real. No man could hold back an angel, no good angel would hold back an angel, so this prince of Persia is a demon lord who went to war with an angel of God. The fact that he is called the **prince** of Persia lets us know that demon lords are assigned positions of power over world kingdoms. How powerful was this demon? How fierce was the warfare? Michael, the warrior angel of God, had to come and turn the tide of battle. In Genesis 3, we see angels carrying flaming swords. What must this conflict have been like?

The **kings** of Persia were the literal human rulers of Persia. We see this by comparing the first verse of the next chapter, where the angel says that he *also* stood to strengthen Darius. You see, it was under the kings of Persia that the Jews were allowed to go home. They were doing what God desired, and the devil was fighting it. This type of warfare still goes on, unseen, in and about the rulers of men today.

Daniel 10:14 *Now I am come to make thee understand what shall befall thy people in the latter days: for yet the vision is for many days.* **15** *And when he had spoken such words unto me, I set my face toward the ground, and I became dumb.*

Notice this carefully. Daniel had enough experience with visions and dreams to know that his vision was for the latter days. That was no surprise to him. What was such a surprise that he could not speak, was the fact that the very demons of Hell were at that moment warring against the angels of God and the people of God, and that his prayers were at the center of it. If a person ever wants to make Heaven cheer and Hell scream, he will go to serious prayer.

Daniel 10:16 *And, behold, one like the similitude of the sons of men touched my lips: then I opened my mouth, and spake, and said unto him that stood before me, O my lord, by the vision my sorrows are turned upon me, and I have retained no strength.* **17** *For how can the servant of this my lord talk with this my lord? for as for me, straightway there remained no strength in me, neither is there breath left in me.*

The mention of the spiritual warfare silenced Daniel, but the vision itself sorrowed him. When he was touched and could finally speak, he gave us a preview one more time of how hard things are going to be in the last days.

Daniel 10:18 *Then there came again and touched me one like the appearance of a man, and he strengthened me,* **19** *And said, O man greatly beloved, fear not: peace be unto thee, be strong, yea, be strong. And when he had spoken unto me, I was strengthened, and said, Let my lord speak; for thou hast strengthened me.*

Do you not just love the fact that God will reach down and touch you more than once? Sometimes, you just need more than one touch from our loving God. The first touch gave Daniel back his speech. The second touch gave Daniel back his strength.

Daniel 10:20 *Then said he, Knowest thou wherefore I come unto thee?* **(The answer was yes. Daniel now knew that this angel had come from heaven, and gone right**

173

through a demonic hornet's nest in the atmosphere to get to him) *and now will I return to fight with the prince of Persia: and when I am gone forth, lo, the prince of Grecia shall come.* **21** *But I will shew thee that which is noted in the scripture of truth: and there is none that holdeth with me in these things, but Michael your prince.*

Do you remember what the devil is?

Ephesians 2:2 *Wherein in time past ye walked according to the course of this world, according to **the prince of the power of the air**, the spirit that now worketh in the children of disobedience:*

In order for an angel to get from Heaven to Earth or Earth to Heaven, he has to go right through the devil's living room. And this angel who had already gone through round one was going back for more, and you get the feeling that when he says *Now will I return to fight*, he was looking forward to it. He was going to vanquish the demon lord of Persia, and Persia the kingdom was going to fall. But Greece was coming in and with it would come a new demon lord.

I do not know how the odds always are, but in this case, it would be two angels against who knows how many demons. Michael and whoever this other angel was were going back to war. I wonder how Daniel prayed that night, knowing that while he slept, fiery swords were clashing?

Chapter 13

Mystery, Murder, and Mayhem in the Middle East - Part 1

Note: Previously in this book material has been footnoted individually. In Daniel 11, most of the material in each point is taken from too many sources to be able to give individual credit to any one. Major sources used include Adam Clarke; Matthew Henry; Jamison, Fausset, and Brown; Willmington's Guide to the Old Testament; Hutchings on Daniel; and several minor sources as well.

Daniel 11:1 *Also I in the first year of Darius the Mede, even I, stood to confirm and to strengthen him.* **2** *And now will I shew thee the truth. Behold, there shall stand up yet three kings in Persia; and the fourth shall be far richer than they all: and by his strength through his riches he shall stir up all against the realm of Grecia.* **3** *And a mighty king shall stand up, that shall rule with great dominion, and do according to his will.* **4** *And when he shall stand up, his kingdom shall be broken, and shall be divided toward the four winds of heaven; and not to his posterity, nor according to his dominion which* *he ruled: for his kingdom shall be plucked up, even for others beside those. 5 And the king of the south shall be strong, and one of his princes; and he shall be strong above him, and have dominion; his dominion shall be a great dominion. 6 And in the end of years they shall join themselves together; for the king's daughter of the south shall come to the king of the north to make an agreement: but she shall not retain the power of the arm; neither shall he stand, nor his arm: but she shall be given up, and they that brought her, and he that begat her, and he that strengthened her in these times. 7 But out of a branch of her roots shall one stand up in his estate, which shall come with an army, and shall enter into the fortress of the king of the north, and shall deal against them, and shall prevail: 8 And shall also carry captives into Egypt their gods, with their princes, and with their precious vessels of silver and of gold; and he shall continue more years than the king of the north. 9 So the king of the south shall come into his kingdom, and shall return into his own land. 10 But his sons shall be stirred up, and shall assemble a multitude of great forces: and one shall certainly come, and overflow, and pass through: then shall he return, and be stirred up, even to his fortress. 11 And the king of the south shall be moved with choler, and shall come forth and fight with him, even with the king of the north: and he shall set forth a great multitude; but the multitude shall be given into his hand. 12 And when he hath taken away the multitude, his heart shall be lifted up; and he shall cast down many ten thousands: but he shall not be strengthened by it. 13 For the king of the north shall return, and shall set forth a multitude greater than the former, and shall certainly come after certain years with a great army and with much riches.*

Chapter eleven will be another example of the breathtaking nature of the book of Daniel, but it will do so in a much different style. Much of the prophecies we have seen thus far have dealt with kings and kingdoms. Chapter eleven, which at forty-five verses is the second longest chapter in the entire book, will give minute details of amazing intrigue involving politically arranged marriages, alliances formed and broken, double crossing left and right, and small people who did things to change the world. It will do so in such detail that looking back at history, any honest person will have to be convinced that the Bible is indeed the very Word of God.

A Money-Driven War

Daniel 11:1 *Also I in the first year of Darius the Mede, even I, stood to confirm and to strengthen him.* **2** *And now will I shew thee the truth. Behold, there shall stand up yet three kings in Persia; and the fourth shall be far richer than they all: and by his strength through his riches he shall stir up all against the realm of Grecia.*

As the chapter begins, the angel reminds Daniel that he had been there to strengthen Darius in his decision to extend kindness to the Jews. But from that point, this angel comes back around to Daniel and promises to show him the truth concerning things to come. The angel told him that there were four kings left to come in Persia, and that the fourth one would be richer than the other three before him. That is a very specific prophecy. How did it work out?

Cyrus was the king at the time of this prophecy according to Daniel 10:1. After Cyrus, came a king named Cambyses. After Cambyses came Peudo-Smerdis, and after Smerdis came Darius Hystaspis. (Aslo known in Ezra 4:6, 7, 24 as Ahasuerus, Artaxerxes, and Darius) That makes three. After Darius Hystaspis came Xerxes. That makes four, just as Daniel's prophecy says.

What about the part that says the fourth would be richer than the first three? History is clear that the kings before Xerxes handled the finances of the kingdom very well, so by the time Xerxes came to the throne the treasury was bulging. He was indeed richer than those who came before him. But did you notice how the Bible said he would use that money?

...and by his strength through his riches he shall stir up all against the realm of Grecia.

Did this come true? History says that it did. Xerxes used that money to equip an army of two million men to conquer the area we now know as Europe. They had the best equipment and innovations money could buy. In fact, one thing they pioneered during this campaign is still used even by our own military today. His army corp of engineers placed ships side by side across the straits of Thermopylae into Greece. His army marched across with dry feet to go to battle. It took seven days for all two million soldiers to get across!

Persia had overwhelming numbers, but the tiny Greek army put up an unbelievable fight. The Persians never could completely destroy the Greeks, and that was eventually going to come back to haunt them.

A Menacing Backlash

Daniel 11:3 *And a mighty king shall stand up, that shall rule with great dominion, and do according to his will.*

According to what we see in the next verse, this verse is clearly another prophecy of the rise of Alexander the Great. When Alexander came to rule Greece, he remembered well what Persia did with all of that money, hiring and equipping that two million man army against them. That helps to make what we read in Daniel 8:7 make even more sense:

Daniel 8:7 *And I saw him* (**Alexander**) *come close unto the ram* (**Persia**)*, and he was moved with choler against him, and smote the ram, and brake his two horns: and there was no power in the ram to stand before him, but he cast him down to the ground, and stamped upon him: and there was none that could deliver the ram out of his hand.*

Alexander hated Persia, hated her past rulers, and hated her present rulers. If you remember chapter eight you remember that with Alexander, this was intensely personal. History records Alexander as a man that did not like to be challenged. He felt like everyone should do what he said, the very moment he said it, and give him whatever he wanted, the moment he wanted it. But there was an enemy general that had no intentions of bowing to the "upstart" Alexander. Darius Codomannus was the Emperor of Persia, and commander of the armies. He intended to stop Alexander in his tracks, and

178

he tried it three times. Each time, as was the normal way of the Persians, he committed huge numbers of soldiers to the field, dwarfing what Alexander had to work with. Alexander did not take that as a normal part of battle; he took it as a personal insult. He literally got enraged at the thought of it. Let me remind you how remarkable the rise of Alexander the Great was. He had an army of about 30,000 men and 5,000 horses. He was fighting against a Medo-Persian army estimated to be nearly a million strong. He was facing overwhelming odds in manpower.

Three times these two armies met, three times Alexander and Darius Codomannus matched leadership skills. In all three battles, fought at Granicus, Issus, and Arbela, the tiny army of Alexander routed the massive army of the Persians. In the last battle alone, the Grecians wiped out some 600,000 soldiers of the Persians.[11] That crippled them and ruined them as a world power. That battle determined the history of the Middle East for the next two hundred years.

A Memorable Division

Daniel 11:4 *And when he shall stand up* (**when he conquers everything**)*, his kingdom shall be broken, and shall be divided toward the four winds of heaven; and not to his posterity, nor according to his dominion which he ruled: for his kingdom shall be plucked up, even for others beside those.* **5** *And the king of the south shall be strong, and one of his princes; and he shall be strong above him, and have dominion; his dominion shall be a great dominion.*

Some of this we have already seen, such as the part about Alexander being broken and his kingdom split in four pieces and none of it going to his posterity. After a drunken binge, Alexander died at age thirty-three at the height of his power. His empire was then split into four parts, with each of his generals taking one part. Cassander got Macedonia and Greece, Lysimachus got Asia Minor, Seleucus got Syria and Babylonia, and Ptolemy got Egypt and North Africa.

179

But here is where chapter eleven gets even more specific. It says that:

...the king of the south shall be strong, and one of his princes; and he shall be strong above him, and have dominion; his dominion shall be a great dominion.

Does history record anything like this? As a matter of fact it does. Ptolemy, ruling Egypt, was the one that this verse calls *the king of the South.* He ruled Egypt well and did indeed become very strong. The one of his princes that became strong was Seleucus, the vice regent of Babylonia. A man named Antigonus conspired against Seleucus, and Seleucus had to flee into Egypt to his friend Ptolemy. Ptolemy made him a prince in his empire and financed a military conquest for him to retake Babylon.

Notice that verse five prophesied that Seluecus would become even greater than Ptolomy. That happened as well. After regaining Babylon with Ptolemy's help, Seleucus went on to conquer from India to Syria and Assyria. His dominion became far greater than the dominion of Ptolemy in Egypt. Everything happened exactly as God said it would.

A Mysterious Plot

Daniel 11:6 *And in the end of years they shall join themselves together; for the king's daughter of the south shall come to the king of the north to make an agreement: but she shall not retain the power of the arm; neither shall he stand, nor his arm: but she shall be given up, and they that brought her, and he that begat her, and he that strengthened her in these times.*

In every good mystery there has to be a mysterious woman. Guys are many things, but they are not one bit mysterious...

Ladies, here is a part for you in this story. Verse six speaks of the fact that the king's daughter of the south would come to the king of the north to make an agreement. Years after Ptolemy and Seleucus had done their dance, it was decided that it would be to the advantage of both Syria and

Egypt for there to be an alliance. So Bernice, the daughter of the king of the South, was given by Ptolemy II of Egypt to Antiochus Theos of Syria. The catch to this was that Antiochus had to divorce his own wife Laodice and proclaim that her two children by him were actually the illegitimate offspring of another man!

Do you have an idea what Ptolemy II was trying to accomplish? He was trying to double cross Antiochus and take his kingdom. Once the children of Laodice were tagged as "illegitimate" they could not have the throne. Whatever kids his daughter Bernice had would then be king, and since they would be babies, it would be as simple as bumping off Antiochus, and he would be in control of both of their kingdoms, which he could then merge into one. But shortly after this arranged marriage, shortly after the divorce and the claim of illegitimacy, Ptolemy II, Bernice's father, died. At that point, Antiochus Theos demoted Bernice to the status of a concubine and brought back Laodice as his wife again.

Can you imagine how that went over? "Hey honey! My new wife's dad just died. I've decided to make her a concubine and bring you back as my wife again. Sorry about that 'your kids are illegitimate' thing. No hard feelings, right?"

Well apparently she did have some hard feelings, verse six said:

...she **(Bernice, the new wife/concubine)** *shall not retain the power of the arm; neither shall he* **(Antiochus Theos, the worthless husband)** *stand, nor his arm*:

Let me tell you how this part of the verse was fulfilled. Laodice, the jealous, furious old wife/new wife again, murdered both her husband and Bernice! Hearing of that, Bernice's brother Eurgetes set out to avenge his sister's death. He ransacked Syria and took home a fortune in gold, silver, and other materials. This is exactly what the next three verses are talking about.

Daniel 11:7 *But out of a branch of her roots* **(her brother, Eurgetes)** *shall one stand up in his estate, which shall come with an army, and shall enter into the fortress of the* *king of the north, and shall deal against them, and shall prevail:* **8** *And shall also carry captives into Egypt their gods, with their princes, and with their precious vessels of silver and of gold; and he shall continue more years than the king of the north.* **9** *So the king of the south shall come into his kingdom, and shall return into his own land.*

Jerome wrote that Eurgetes brought back forty thousand talents of silver, four thousand talents of gold, and two thousand costly statues. Needless to say, that only served to stir up the bitterness between these two kingdoms.

A Murderous March

Daniel 11:10 *But his* **(Antiochus Theos')** *sons shall be stirred up, and shall assemble a multitude of great forces: and one shall certainly come, and overflow, and pass through: then shall he return, and be stirred up, even to his fortress.* **11** *And the king of the south* **(Ptolemy Philopater, King of Egypt)** *shall be moved with choler, and shall come forth and fight with him, even with the king of the north: and he* **(Antiochus)** *shall set forth a great multitude; but the multitude shall be given into his* **(Ptolemy's)** *hand.*

After the beating that Syria took at the hands of Egypt and all the great financial loss, the sons of Antiochus Theos and the sons of some former Syrian rulers put aside their differences, banded together, and determined to march against Egypt. By this time another Ptolemy was on the throne, Ptolemy Philopater, and another Antiochus had gotten control of the Syrian forces. In 218 B.C., they attacked the Egyptian fortress at Gaza. This should have been an overwhelming win for Syria. But history records that the Egyptians at Gaza managed to hold the Syrians off long enough for Philopater to gather his entire army. Without the element of surprise on their side, the fresher and better supplied Egyptians won, just as this verse prophesied hundreds of years before it happened.

182

A Mistake in Judgment

Daniel 11:12 *And when he* (**Ptolemy**) *hath taken away the multitude, his heart shall be lifted up; and he shall cast down many ten thousands: but he shall not be strengthened by it.* **13** *For the king of the north shall return, and shall set forth a multitude greater than the former, and shall certainly come after certain years with a great army and with much riches.*

Let me tell you what history records that perfectly matches the prophecy of these verses. The verse says that when he, Ptolemy Philopater, hath taken away the multitude, his heart would be lifted up and he would cast down many ten thousands. He did just that. Enraged at the attack from Syria, Ptolemy ordered tens of thousands of captives to be slaughtered. Had he followed through by marching on Syria, he would have destroyed them completely and never had to worry about it again. But history records Ptolemy as fancying himself as somewhat of a playboy rather than a soldier. So instead of following through, he made Antiochus promise to behave and sent him away in peace. That is why verse twelve says that Ptolemy would not be strengthened by his victory. He let the enemy get away. And verse thirteen prophesied that he would pay the price for it.

And that is exactly what happened. The king of the North did return. In fact, as soon as he got home, he started immediately rebuilding his forces and plotting another attack against Egypt.

This all seems like a history lesson! But it is God's Word, which means that God expects us to pay attention and learn some things from it, so here goes. One, the Bible is not like any other book. Two, use your money for good. Had Xerxes not used his wealth for war to make more wealth, none of this would have happened. Three, you will reap what you sow. What Xerxes did led to the rise of Alexander the Great and the destruction of the Persian Empire many years later. Four, be ready for eternity. If death could take Alexander the Great at the height of his power, it can take you at the height of yours. Five, ladies, be careful who you marry. Bernice got a real creep in Antiochus Theos! Six, men, be careful how you treat your wife. Antiochus got what he had coming to him when Laodice struck back. You have to sleep sometime! Seven, never trust the enemy to behave.

Chapter 14

Mystery, Murder, and Mayhem in the Middle East - Part 2

Note: Previously in this book material has been footnoted individually. In Daniel 11, most of the material in each point is taken from too many sources to be able to give individual credit to any one. Major sources used include Adam Clarke; Matthew Henry; Jamison, Fausset, and Brown; Willmington's Guide to the Old Testament; Hutchings on Daniel; and several minor sources as well.

Daniel 11:14 *And in those times there shall many stand up against the king of the south: also the robbers of thy people shall exalt themselves to establish the vision; but they shall fall.* **15** *So the king of the north shall come, and cast up a mount, and take the most fenced cities: and the arms of the south shall not withstand, neither his chosen people, neither shall there be any strength to withstand.* **16** *But he that cometh against him shall do according to his own will, and none shall stand before him: and he shall stand in the glorious land, which by his hand shall be consumed.* **17** *He shall also set his face to enter with*

the strength of his whole kingdom, and upright ones with him;
thus shall he do: and he shall give him the daughter of women,
corrupting her: but she shall not stand on his side, neither be
for him. **18** *After this shall he turn his face unto the isles, and*
shall take many: but a prince for his own behalf shall cause the
reproach offered by him to cease; without his own reproach he
shall cause it to turn upon him. **19** *Then he shall turn his face*
toward the fort of his own land: but he shall stumble and fall,
and not be found. **20** *Then shall stand up in his estate a raiser*
of taxes in the glory of the kingdom: but within few days he
shall be destroyed, neither in anger, nor in battle.

Trouble in Egypt

Daniel 11:14 *And in those times there shall many stand*
up against the king of the south: also the robbers of thy people
shall exalt themselves to establish the vision; but they shall fall.

When Ptolemy Philopater was on the throne in Egypt,
he demonstrated some kindness to the Jews. You see, his
father, the brother of Bernice, was a Godly man and even came
and worshipped in Jerusalem. So even though Philopater was
not Godly, he did have some good will toward the Jews
because of his father. Philopater, knowing people that were
good with money when he saw them, turned over the entire
business affairs of Egypt to the Jews. Thousands of Jews then
moved from Israel to Alexandria, Egypt, to become merchants.

But as has been true throughout history, things will
never go permanently well for the Jews among the nations of
the world. After Philopater died, a new king took the throne,
and he decided to kill the Jews. What was his motive? Verse
fourteen tells us quite clearly: he was a "robber of thy people."
He wanted to seize their wealth. That was his "vision." Kill
the Jews; rob them. But notice that verse fourteen prophesied
that they would exalt themselves to establish that vision, but
they would fall. Is that how things happened? The Jewish
historian Josephus records that all of the Jews in Alexandria
were gathered together in the town square and stripped naked.

186

Elephants belonging to the Egyptian army were first made drunk and then turned loose to trample the Jews.

Now, does anyone besides me see a flaw in that plan? Like, for instance, how successful do you think you will be getting drunken elephants to do what you want them to do?

The drunken elephants did not trample and kill the Jews. Instead, in their confusion and fury, they turned on their handlers and the soldiers and killed a bunch of them!

Two on One

Daniel 11:15 *So the king of the north shall come, and cast up a mount, and take the most fenced cities: and the arms of the south shall not withstand, neither his chosen people, neither shall there be any strength to withstand. **16** But he that cometh against him shall do according to his own will, and none shall stand before him: and he shall stand in the glorious land, which by his hand shall be consumed.*

Do you remember what Antiochus began to do as soon as he got back home from his loss to Egypt and Ptolemy? He broke his promise and began to rebuild his army to go to war with them once again. Verse fifteen and sixteen tell of that second battle. In order for Antiochus the Great to get to Egypt, he first had to get through Israel, which was sandwiched right between them. Israel was under Egyptian domination but also under Egyptian protection. Because Israel was not allowed by Egypt to have an army, a garrison of Egyptian soldiers was there to protect them. As Antiochus marched against Israel, Ptolemy sent Scopus to lead the forces against them. Scopus and Egypt were defeated near the fountains of Jordan,[12] and as verse sixteen prophesied, Antiochus did indeed come and stand *in the glorious land.*

But notice also that verse sixteen said that when Antiochus came into the land it would be consumed by his hand. The resources of the land were wasted and ruined by that war between Egypt and Syria that happened in Israel. Daniel is right on the verge of seeing his people go back from captivity and rebuild, and he is being told that one more time,

187

the land would be ravaged. Sadly, it would not be the last time an Antiochus ravaged Israel.

But as Antiochus the Great stood in Israel, the Glorious Land, readying himself to march against Egypt, he got some news. The Egyptians had signed a treaty of mutual aid with a new nation rising to power in the West. It was not going to be a one-on-one battle, Syria versus Egypt, it was going to be a two-on-one battle. You might be interested in the name of that newcomer to the battle, that emerging world power. The name that Antiochus was hearing that made him so nervous was Rome.

Twists and Turns

Daniel 11:17 *He shall also set his face to enter with the strength of his whole kingdom, and upright ones with him; thus shall he do: and he shall give him the daughter of women, corrupting her: but she shall not stand on his side, neither be for him.*

This one little verse is just loaded, so hang on tight. We read first that Antiochus would *set his face to enter with the strength of his whole kingdom.* Not his whole *army,* his whole *kingdom.* In other words, Antiochus was thinking way bigger than anyone realized. He knew that if it was military versus military, his chances were iffy since the Romans were now involved. So instead of bringing his entire army to war against Egypt, he intended to bring his kingdom into Egypt, and make both kingdoms his. Before we get to *how* he intended to do it, let's focus on *how he intended to look* while doing it. Verse seventeen uses this phrase, *and upright ones with him.* That is a Hebrew figure of speech that basically means, "He would act as though he had the best of intentions." Think of our own government today for an example:

We're only taking your guns because bad guys may take them from you and hurt you. Trust us, we'll take care of you.

We're not going to tax you, we're going to tax the rich! And then we're going to give you that money in the form of government programs. Trust us, we'll take goooood care of you.

Yes, we're taking away your freedoms one by one, but after all, it's all for the children. If you oppose a government that acts like a great big nanny, why, you must be anti-child! Trust us, it's all for your own good that we're doing this...

That is the approach that Antiochus the Great took. When he came into Egypt, he left the army behind in Israel and came as an ambassador of goodwill. And he did not come empty handed; he had "bait" with him. The "bait" was his seven-year-old daughter Cleopatra. (A different Cleopatra from the one you know of with Marc Antony, she was about a hundred years later.)

The monarch of Egypt at the time was also seven years old, a little boy named Ptolemy Epiphanes. Antiochus proposed that the royal households of Egypt and Syria be united by a marriage between these two children. That is what verse seventeen means when it says he would *give him the daughter of women*. But notice that it does not stop there. Look at the next two words, *corrupting her*. Daddy corrupted his own daughter for his own selfish ends. He filled her mind with deceit and double-crossing. He taught her that when she was old enough to consummate the marriage, she should get control of the kingdom from her young husband and give it over to him. She was to use her sexuality as a tool to get something by deceit. At twelve years old, the marriage finally took place and was consummated. It was at that point that daddy Antiochus was sitting back, waiting for word to come that she had gotten the kingdom for him.

Now let me ask a second time: does anyone but me see a flaw in this plan? The only thing harder to control than a bunch of drunken elephants is a deceitful twelve-year-old girl! Cleopatra learned deceit very well from her father, and she decided to use it against him! She told her young husband about her father's plans to take Egypt. He then contacted his new ally, the Romans, and had them attack a bunch of Syrian ships. When the Romans defeated her father's ships, little Cleopatra sent them congratulations on their victory over her father! That is an absolute perfect fulfillment of the end of verse seventeen:

...but she **(Cleopatra)** *shall not stand on his* **(her father Antiochus)** *side, neither be for him.*

Be careful what you teach your kids!

Daniel 11:18 *After this shall he turn his face unto the isles, and shall take many: but a prince for his own behalf shall cause the reproach offered by him to cease; without his own reproach he shall cause it to turn upon him.* **19** *Then he shall turn his face toward the fort of his own land: but he shall stumble and fall, and not be found.*

Once the Romans started attacking Syrian ships, Antiochus turned his focus to them. He outfitted three hundred warships to fight against Rome and plunder her ports. That is the fulfillment of the first part of verse eighteen; *he shall turn his face to the isles, and shall take many.*

But the verse next prophesied a prince that would end the reproach brought on Rome by Antiochus. That prince was a young man of Caesar's household named Scipio. He led a fleet against the ships of Antiochus and won big. So crushing was this defeat that Antiochus returned to Antioch and sent an ambassador to Rome asking for terms of peace. That is a perfect fulfillment of verse nineteen that he would *turn his face toward the fort of his own land.* But did you notice what would happen after he got back home, after he sent that ambassador asking for terms of peace? It says *but he shall stumble and fall, and not be found.* Let me tell you about the fulfilment of that.

The terms of peace that Rome laid down were brutal. Antiochus had to give up all of his holdings in Europe and much of Western Turkey. But that was not all. Rome would grant him peace only on condition of paying the expense of the war, fifteen thousand talents; five hundred on the spot, two thousand five hundred when the peace should be ratified by the senate, and the remaining twelve thousand in twelve years, each year one thousand.[13]

That was an astronomical sum. The only way he could think of to pay it was by robbing the temples of his false gods. But while robbing the Temple of Bel in Elymais, he was killed, perfectly fulfilling the end of verse nineteen.

Taxed to Death

Daniel 11:20 *Then shall stand up in his estate a raiser of taxes in the glory of the kingdom: but within few days he shall be destroyed, neither in anger, nor in battle.*

After Antiochus died, his oldest son Seleucus Philopater took the throne. The problem was, the debt that the Romans laid on Syria was still in effect. Seleucus had to find some way to pay the debt that his father died trying to pay. He knew from his father's death that robbing the temples at home was not a safe idea. So instead, just as verse twenty prophesied, he imposed a heavy tax on the Jews in the glorious kingdom of Israel.

The last payment was coming due, and Seleucus saw that he was not going to make it even with all the taxes on the Jews. So he sent his treasurer to Jerusalem to take all of the gold from the Temple. He should not have done that. God does not take it lightly when His man or His house is assaulted.

Notice that the end of the verse says that within a few days he would be destroyed, *neither in anger nor in battle.* Was that fulfilled? Well, he did not die at war leading the armies. He did not die from some angry subject openly assassinating him. He died very quietly, actually. One day he was as healthy as could be, the next day he just mysteriously started getting sick and next thing you know, out of the blue, he was dead. Poison tends to do that to you. His own treasurer quietly poisoned him to steal the wealth that he had stolen from others.

Do you see yet again how unique the Bible is? There is no book like the Bible!

Let's close this chapter like we did the last one, with a few practical applications. One, never turn against the Jews. You may find yourself under an elephant or two. Two, just because someone claims to have your best interests at heart does not make it so. Egypt found that out when dealing with sneaky Antiochus. Three, teach your children honesty and righteousness, not deceit. If you teach them wrong, they may one day line up against you! Four, when you get married, your first human responsibility is your spouse. Cleopatra got that one right! Five, never line up against the House of God or a real Man of God.

Chapter 15

Mystery, Murder, and Mayhem in the Middle East - Part 3

Note: Previously in this book material has been footnoted individually. In Daniel 11, most of the material in each point is taken from too many sources to be able to give individual credit to any one. Major sources used include Adam Clarke; Matthew Henry; Jamison, Fausset, and Brown; Willmington's Guide to the Old Testament; Hutchings on Daniel; and several minor sources as well.

Daniel 11:21 *And in his estate shall stand up a vile person, to whom they shall not give the honour of the kingdom: but he shall come in peaceably, and obtain the kingdom by flatteries.* **22** *And with the arms of a flood shall they be overflown from before him, and shall be broken; yea, also the prince of the covenant.* **23** *And after the league made with him he shall work deceitfully: for he shall come up, and shall become strong with a small people.* **24** *He shall enter peaceably even upon the fattest places of the province; and he shall do that which his fathers have not done, nor his fathers'*

fathers; he shall scatter among them the prey, and spoil, and riches: yea, and he shall forecast his devices against the strong holds, even for a time. 25 And he shall stir up his power and his courage against the king of the south with a great army; and the king of the south shall be stirred up to battle with a very great and mighty army; but he shall not stand: for they shall forecast devices against him. 26 Yea, they that feed of the portion of his meat shall destroy him, and his army shall overflow: and many shall fall down slain. 27 And both these kings' hearts shall be to do mischief, and they shall speak lies at one table; but it shall not prosper: for yet the end shall be at the time appointed. 28 Then shall he return into his land with great riches; and his heart shall be against the holy covenant; and he shall do exploits, and return to his own land. 29 At the time appointed he shall return, and come toward the south; but it shall not be as the former, or as the latter. 30 For the ships of Chittim shall come against him: therefore he shall be grieved, and return, and have indignation against the holy covenant: so shall he do; he shall even return, and have intelligence with them that forsake the holy covenant. 31 And arms shall stand on his part, and they shall pollute the sanctuary of strength, and shall take away the daily sacrifice, and they shall place the abomination that maketh desolate.

The Coming Peacemaker

Daniel 11:21 *And in his estate shall stand up a vile person, to whom they shall not give the honour of the kingdom: but he shall come in peaceably, and obtain the kingdom by flatteries.*

After Seleucus Philopater was poisoned to death, the next in line for the throne was his son Demetrius. But Demetrius, the son of Seleucus Philopater, never made it to the throne. His uncle, Seleucus' brother, took the throne instead, and he is the person spoken of in this verse. You've probably never heard of Demetrius who was supposed to be king. But I guarantee you that you have heard of the man who stole the throne from him. He was yet another Antiochus. The

194

Antiochus.   Antiochus Epiphanes, the little horn, the
forerunner in type of the Antichrist.

When Seleucus died, Antiochus went to work to seize
the throne. Notice that this verse foretold that this vile, wicked
man would also be a peacemaker and would obtain the
kingdom by flatteries. That prophecy was perfectly, flawlessly
fulfilled. He needed an army, so he flattered Eumenes, King
of Pergamus, and Attalus his brother and got their assistance.
The Romans ruled the world, so he flattered them and even
payed the back taxes that his predecessors owed them.   He
flattered the Syrians so much that they gave him the nickname
of Epiphanes – the Illustrious.   He even outdid modern
politicians: he went into the markets and flattered all the
common workers, then went into the taverns and boozed it up
with the drunks.   Whoever you were, Antiochus made you
actually believe you were the greatest thing living to him. He
was the living embodiment of the old phrase "Be very sincere
when you fake sincerity."   When he was done with all that
flattery, Demetrius had been exiled and Antiochus was king.

Daniel 11:22 *And with the arms of a flood shall they be
overflown from before him, and shall be broken; yea, also the
prince of the covenant.*

The "they" spoken of here refers to the competitors he
had for the throne, Demetrius and those who were with him.
They were *overflown by a flood and broken.* In other words,
Antiochus and his gang just rolled over them. But they were
not the only ones that drowned in the flood that was Antiochus
Epiphanes. This verse also tells us that another was going to
be broken, one called *the prince of the covenant.*

As far as history is concerned, this was fulfilled when
Antiochus put out the Jewish high priest Onias III and replaced
him with a man who bribed him for the job, a man named
Jason. But you know, there really is no honor among thieves.
When another man named Menelaus offered him an even
bigger bribe, Antiochus put Jason out in favor of him! As far
as prophecy is concerned, remember that Antiochus is the
forerunner in type of Antichrist to come. So a whole bunch of

195

what we will see in this passage about Antiochus will be fulfilled in even greater measure in Antichrist. Antiochus came against the prince of the covenant, Antichrist will try to defeat the Prince of Peace, our Great High Priest, Jesus.

Daniel 11:23 *And after the league made with him he shall work deceitfully: for he shall come up, and shall become strong with a small people.*

The league spoken of here was between Antiochus Epiphanes and Ptolemy Philometer of Egypt. There is a reason why you might think that these two could keep a treaty; they were related! Antiochus was the uncle of Ptolemy.[14] But this was a family in which if members were hugging each other, they were probably looking for a good place to stick the knife. That would later be the case with these two as we shall see in just a bit. But Antiochus was by far the better criminal, and he ended up stealing control of Egypt from his nephew. He started with such a small force but was a major force before you could blink an eye. And he did it all by *peace.* His weapon was flattery rather than fireworks. The next verse bears that out again:

Daniel 11:24 *He shall enter peaceably even upon the fattest places of the province; and he shall do that which his fathers have not done, nor his fathers' fathers; he shall scatter among them the prey, and spoil, and riches: yea, and he shall forecast his devices against the strong holds, even for a time.*

Just by talking, Antiochus ended up in control of places like Coelesyria, Palestine, and others. His riches grew exponentially, and when they did, this shrewd politician did something that verse twenty-four says none of his forefathers were shrewd enough to do. Those who came before him were after wealth for wealth's sake. What they got, they kept. Antiochus was after power. Notice that the verse says he would scatter his spoils and riches. Antiochus was buying people's loyalty, and he did it with flair. He would sometimes go into the streets and throw out a handful of money, crying out, "Let him take it, to whom fortune sends it."

196

Now remember that a lot of that money Antiochus was throwing around came from his takeover of Egypt. But the young Egyptian king, Ptolemy Philometer, had two guardians named Eulaeus and Lenaeus. They demanded from Antiochus the restitution of Coelesyria and Palestine. Naturally he refused, at which point he foresaw that he might have a war with that kingdom. But Antiochus was never one to fight on equal terms, so as the verse says he "forecast devices" against them. He visited the strong holds and frontier places to see that they were in a state of defense and for several years prepared for battle against Egypt. He was about to move from *Coming Peacemaker* to *Conquering Prince*.

The Conquering Prince

Daniel 11:25 *And he shall stir up his power and his courage against the king of the south with a great army; and the king of the south shall be stirred up to battle with a very great and mighty army; but he shall not stand: for they shall forecast devices against him.* **26** *Yea, they that feed of the portion of his meat shall destroy him, and his army shall overflow: and many shall fall down slain.*

Remember that Antiochus Epiphanes is the King of Syria, the king of the north, and Ptolemy Philometer his nephew is the King of Egypt, the king of the south. When it finally came time to put flatteries aside and go to all-out war, it was a big one. Both North and South had large forces, but Antiochus had something that Ptolemy did not have. He was an underhanded devil who had already bribed a bunch of his enemy's closest captains and advisors. Just as verse twenty-six says, people who were eating at Ptolemy's own table betrayed him. Egypt got routed by an outward enemy because they had first been corrupted from within.

Antiochus was able to conquer all of Egypt except Alexandria. The Alexandrians then made Ptolemy's brother, Eurgetes, king in his place.

197

The Corrupt Pairing

Daniel 11:27 *And both these kings' hearts shall be to do mischief, and they shall speak lies at one table; but it shall not prosper: for yet the end shall be at the time appointed.*

Remember how we talked about uncle and nephew both looking for a place to stick the knife? This verse prophesies that. When the battle was over and Antiochus and his nephew "kissed and made up," Antiochus and Philometer would often sit down and talk about how awful it was that the Alexandrians had been so bad to Philometer. Uncle Antiochus would talk about all the ways that he could help his little nephew (whose kingdom he had stolen), and Philometer would go on at length about how grateful he was for all his dear uncle's help (whom he hated). Like this verse says, they were at the same table speaking lies. Both of them had their own interests at heart and their own plans. But neither of them would prosper just yet in their plans, because as the verse says *it shall not prosper, for yet the end shall be at the time appointed.*

It is kind of nice to know that evil still has to abide by God's schedule!

The Curse of Power

Daniel 11:28 *Then shall he return into his land with great riches; and his heart shall be against the holy covenant; and he shall do exploits, and return to his own land.*

This verse and the two to follow are loaded with history. Antiochus did return into his land with great riches; his campaign against Egypt had been a huge success. We would expect for him to be in a really good mood and maybe take a long while to celebrate. But notice that the very next thing that is prophesied of him is that *his heart would be against the holy covenant; and he shall do exploits.* If you think that does not sound good, you are right.

Here is what happened. While Antiochus was in Egypt, a rumor got started in Israel. Someone started saying that Antiochus had died! That report spread like wildfire among the Jews, and they started celebrating in the streets. The problem was, Antiochus was not dead, and he heard about the party. Not too long after, the Jews found out the hard way that he was very much alive. Antiochus Epiphanes came marching into Jerusalem. Before he was done, the historical book of II Maccabees says that he murdered eighty thousand people, took forty thousand prisoners, and sold forty thousand as slaves. His army raped the women, and thousands of Jewish little boys were crucified just because they had been circumcised. Daniel saw all of this before it happened. Can you imagine the tears streaming down old Daniel's face as he listened to this prophecy? And the vision was not even done yet...

The last part of the verse says that Antiochus would return to his own land. But he did not stay there long:

Daniel 11:29 *At the time appointed he shall return, and come toward the south; but it shall not be as the former, or as the latter.*

Remember that when Antiochus was last in Egypt, Alexandria was still resisting him successfully. So Antiochus determined to come against them again. But notice that this time the Bible said his campaign *would not be as the former or the latter.* The former refers to when he overthrew the Egyptian army at Pelusium. The latter referred to when he took Memphis and all of Egypt except Alexandria. Those two were wins for Antiochus Epiphanes. This next campaign was going to be a loss! Here is how it happened, and you are going to love this. Look at verse thirty:

Daniel 11:30a *For the ships of Chittim shall come against him:*

Chittim is an ancient name for Rome. Remember that Rome had previously aligned with Egypt, and now Egypt had enlisted their aid again. Antiochus was coming for Alexandria. But when he and his army arrived, they found a Roman fleet waiting for them in the bay, and it was clearly evident that they could easily beat Antiochus and his forces if they chose to.

Antiochus tried his schmoozing and flattering. He ran up to salute and welcome the Romans, but his reputation had already preceded him. The Romans were not buying any of it. They produced a decree from the Roman senate that he immediately cease any hostilities against Egypt. Slippery Antiochus decided to stall for time. He told the Roman commander that he would have to go and consult with his advisors, and that he would get back to them. The Roman commander, a man named Popilius, walked over to Antiochus there on the beach, took his staff, and drew a circle around him. Then he said, "Before you leave that circle, tell me what I need to tell Rome when I get back." For the first time ever, someone had pinned that slippery snake down, and he had to bow. Antiochus had been overpowered by Rome. But even though he was not as powerful as Rome, he was still more powerful than Israel. Why do I mention that? Because the curse of power is that if you are a complete jerk, you will always find someone weaker than you to take your frustrations out on. Look at the rest of verse thirty and verse thirty-one:

Daniel 11:30b... *therefore he shall be grieved, and return, and have indignation against the holy covenant: so shall he do; he shall even return, and have intelligence with them that forsake the holy covenant. 31 And arms shall stand on his part, and they shall pollute the sanctuary of strength, and shall take away the daily sacrifice, and they shall place the abomination that maketh desolate.*

Antiochus was so upset at being humiliated that he marched into Israel looking for someone to hurt and something to break. Back in verse twenty-eight we were told that he would be *against* the covenant. In verse thirty we are told he would have *indignation against* the covenant. It was going to be far worse the second time around. When Antiochus got back to Israel, he burned the city, tore down houses, killed countless people, and polluted everything he could find. Verse thirty said that he would *have intelligence with them that forsake the holy covenant.* Antiochus bribed a bunch of wicked Jews to spy on their friends and families and anyone else who might try to worship God.

The verse also said that *arms shall stand on his part.* That part of verse thirty-one speaks of the power of the sword that Antiochus had that allowed him to do what he did. And what he did got even worse. See if the last part of verse thirty-one sounds familiar:

...and shall take away the daily sacrifice, and they shall place the abomination that maketh desolate.

Antiochus removed the very altar of God from the Holy of Holies. He set up an altar and an idol of Jupiter. He sacrificed a pig, the most unclean of all animals to a Jew, and he spattered its blood all over that Holy Place where the blood of spotless lambs had so often been lovingly shed for the sins of the people. There was no greater desecration that he could have possibly committed; Antiochus Epiphanes went as low as he could go. The phrase that Daniel used for it here was *the abomination that maketh desolate,* meaning "The filthiness that empties the Holy of Holies of anything worth having."

That phrase should have a familiar ring to it. In fact, it should not be regarded as history to you. Yes, it *was* history, but even to us today, it *is* prophecy. It happened then, but it has not happened yet. Let me show you what I mean:

Matthew 24:15 *When ye therefore shall see **the abomination of desolation**, spoken of by Daniel the prophet, stand in the holy place, (whoso readeth, let him understand:)* **16** *Then let them which be in Judaea flee into the mountains:*

This was Jesus talking, and He was not talking about what did happen under Antiochus Epiphanes; He was talking about what will happen under Antichrist. That is why He said, *Whoso readeth, let him understand.* What Antiochus did, Antichrist will do, only much worse. He will enter the Holy of Holies in the rebuilt Temple in Jerusalem, proclaim himself as god, and command that all the world worship him. This will happen at the mid-way point of the Tribulation Period.

But for now, just leave your thoughts back in the days of what Daniel saw. Jerusalem is ravaged, her homes are burned, dead and mutilated bodies line the streets. In the Temple, the altar of God is in ruins, a false god stands in its place, and the walls and floors are covered with the blood of a pig. It looks as if God has forgotten and forsaken His people. But you hear me well; *God never forgets or forsakes His people.*

Once again, let's make some practical applications in closing. One, never be proud enough or dumb enough to fall for flattery. Two, they say the nut does not fall far from the tree. But if you are from a corrupt tree, fall, roll, do whatever it takes to get as far from the tree as possible! Antiochus and his whole family were corrupt. Three, check your facts before you react. Had the Jews not swallowed the rumor of Antiochus' death, they might not have suffered so much at his hands. Four, remember that no matter how "big and bad" evil is, there is always someone bigger and badder. Antiochus found that out while standing in a circle on the beach. The devil found that out at Calvary! Five, remember that God never forgets or forsakes His people.

Chapter 16

Mystery, Murder, and Mayhem in the Middle East - Part 4

Note: Previously in this book material has been footnoted individually. In Daniel 11, most of the material in each point is taken from too many sources to be able to give individual credit to any one. Major sources used include Adam Clarke; Matthew Henry; Jamison, Fausset, and Brown; Willmington's Guide to the Old Testament; Hutchings on Daniel; and several minor sources as well.

Daniel 11:32 *And such as do wickedly against the covenant shall he corrupt by flatteries: but the people that do know their God shall be strong, and do exploits.* **33** *And they that understand among the people shall instruct many: yet they shall fall by the sword, and by flame, by captivity, and by spoil, many days.* **34** *Now when they shall fall, they shall be holpen with a little help: but many shall cleave to them with flatteries.* **35** *And some of them of understanding shall fall, to try them, and to purge, and to make them white, even to the time of the end: because it is yet for a time appointed.* **36** *And the king* *shall do according to his will; and he shall exalt himself, and magnify himself above every god, and shall speak marvellous things against the God of gods, and shall prosper till the indignation be accomplished: for that that is determined shall be done.* **37** *Neither shall he regard the God of his fathers, nor the desire of women, nor regard any god: for he shall magnify himself above all.* **38** *But in his estate shall he honour the God of forces: and a god whom his fathers knew not shall he honour with gold, and silver, and with precious stones, and pleasant things.* **39** *Thus shall he do in the most strong holds with a strange god, whom he shall acknowledge and increase with glory: and he shall cause them to rule over many, and shall divide the land for gain.* **40** *And at the time of the end shall the king of the south push at him: and the king of the north shall come against him like a whirlwind, with chariots, and with horsemen, and with many ships; and he shall enter into the countries, and shall overflow and pass over.* **41** *He shall enter also into the glorious land, and many countries shall be overthrown: but these shall escape out of his hand, even Edom, and Moab, and the chief of the children of Ammon.* **42** *He shall stretch forth his hand also upon the countries: and the land of Egypt shall not escape.* **43** *But he shall have power over the treasures of gold and of silver, and over all the precious things of Egypt: and the Libyans and the Ethiopians shall be at his steps.* **44** *But tidings out of the east and out of the north shall trouble him: therefore he shall go forth with great fury to destroy, and utterly to make away many.* **45** *And he shall plant the tabernacles of his palace between the seas in the glorious holy mountain; yet he shall come to his end, and none shall help him.*

We have come a long way from the time when Daniel was a teenage kid taken into captivity in Babylon. We have gone through the first six personal chapters and most of the last six prophetical chapters. Chapter eleven itself has been amazing. The details given of what is now history but was prophecy when Daniel wrote it should prove to anyone with a sound mind that the Bible is indeed the very Word of God. The last chapter ended with things looking pretty bad for the people of God and the cause of righteousness. It was all about the wicked man that history calls Antiochus Epiphanes. If you remember, this man was the ruler of Syria. He was a slippery, rotten, flattering liar who did wrong to everyone he came across, even his own family. He stole a throne, a kingdom, and the wealth of many. But Antiochus eventually ran up against the Romans and had to slink away in dishonor.

Enraged at this, he marched into Jerusalem. He had been there before and had killed eighty thousand people, sold forty thousand as slaves, and taken forty thousand as captives. His soldiers had raped the women and crucified little Jewish boys.

The second time he came, after his disgrace at the hands of Rome, he went as low as he could go. He took out his anger on the helpless Jews, burning homes, killing indiscriminately, polluting everything in sight. He then committed what Daniel calls *the abomination that maketh desolate.* He went into the Temple in Jerusalem, destroyed the altar of God, and replaced it with an altar to Jupiter. He then killed a sow and spattered its blood all over the Holy of Holies. He desecrated everything that was sacred to the Jews, and it did not look like he could be stopped. That is where we ended the last chapter.

The Counter-Punch
Daniel 11:32 *And such as do wickedly against the covenant shall he corrupt by flatteries: but the people that do know their God shall be strong, and do exploits.*

Most of what Antiochus did, he did with help from those that should have been his enemies. When he desecrated Jerusalem and the Temple, there were wicked priests and high officials that helped him. Just by flattering them he so corrupted them that they were willing to defile everything that was holy. But thank God that is not the end of the verse or the end of the story. Notice that the last part of the verse starts with "but": *but the people that do know their God shall be strong, and do exploits.* That phrase is a prophecy of a bright spot in Jewish history.

On September 6, 171 B.C., Antiochus started his campaign against the Jews and against the Temple. All throughout Palestine altars were set up to Jupiter, and everyone was commanded to worship them. But in a little town called Modin, seventeen miles northwest of Jerusalem, there was an old Jewish priest named Matthias who had five grown sons. Not only would Matthias not bow to this abomination, he killed the ambassador of Antiochus, then he and his sons started a rebellion. But Mathias was an old man and not fit for a long, raging battle. The war took its toll, and it soon became evident that Mathias was going to die. On his deathbed, he called for his boys and began to prepare them for what was ahead. It was at that point that he passed over his two oldest sons and placed the authority of leading the rebellion on the shoulders of his third son, Judas.

That was an excellent choice. Judas was a strong and capable leader and an expert at guerilla warfare. This was going to be essential, since he was going to be constantly outnumbered. In war it does not take great leaders long to earn a nickname. "Stonewall Jackson." "Unconditional Surrender Grant." Judas also quickly earned a nickname, "Maccabee," which means "Hammer." Judas the Hammer was so great a soldier and leader that he ranks right up there with King David in the hearts and memories of Jews even today!

Mindful of the superiority of Seleucid forces (the Syrian Army) during the first two years of the revolt, the strategy employed by Judas was to avoid any involvement with their regular army and to resort to guerrilla warfare in order to give them a feeling of insecurity. The strategy enabled Judas to win a string of victories. At the battle of Nahal el-Haramiah he defeated a small Syrian force under the command of Apollonius, Governor of Samaria, who was killed. Judas walked over to the dead body and took Apollonius's sword for his own. He used that sword until his death as a symbol of vengeance. After that victory, recruits flocked to the Jewish cause.

A short time later, the Hammer routed a bigger Seleucid army under the command of Seron near Beth-Horon. Then in the Battle of Emmaus he defeated the enemy forces led by Generals Nicanor and Gorgias. At the beginning of the battle, the enemy was closing in and looked as if they would trap Judas' forces. But he led a forced march by night and succeeded in eluding Gorgias, who had intended to attack and destroy the Jewish forces in their camp with his cavalry. While Gorgias was searching for him in the mountains, the Hammer made a surprise attack upon the Seleucid camp and defeated them in the Battle of Emmaus. The Seleucid commander had no alternative but to withdraw to the coast. The defeat at Emmaus convinced General Lysias that he better prepare for a serious and prolonged war. So he assembled a new and larger army and marched with it on Judea from the South via Idumea. But once again, Judas the Maccabee succeeded in overcoming the numerically superior enemy in the battle near Beth-Zur, south of Jerusalem. This victory opened up the road to Jerusalem, so Judas assembled his forces and marched into Jerusalem at the head of his army.

On the 25th of the Jewish month Kislev in 165 B.C., which corresponds to our month of December, the Hammer and his forces recaptured, cleansed, and rededicated the Temple of God. That, friends, is some serious exploits!

But it was not easy. Nothing worth doing ever is.

Daniel 11:33 *And they that understand among the people shall instruct many: yet they shall fall by the sword, and by flame, by captivity, and by spoil, many days.*

Even in the midst of fighting and teaching and trying to guide people into Godliness, good people were still dying by the sword or being burned to death. Good people were still being taken captive and having their possessions taken as spoils. Did you notice that *many days* at the end of the verse? It lasted beyond the time of the Maccabees, beyond the time of the Syrians, even beyond the time of the Romans. In truth, it has not stopped yet and will not until Jesus returns. Pretty much everything from this point until the end of the chapter has one foot in the past and another in the future.

Daniel 11:34 *Now when they shall fall, they shall be holpen with a little help: but many shall cleave to them with flatteries.*

The people falling in this verse is referring back to the Jews suffering under Antiochus. The ones helping them is again talking about Judas and his forces. The obvious reason why Judas and his forces are called *a little help* is because there were not very many of them! But when they started winning, notice that verse twenty-four says *many shall cleave to them with flatteries.* Jewish historians tell us of people like Joseph the son of Zecharias, who was on the enemy's side while they were winning but then flocked to the Maccabee's cause when they started winning!

Daniel 11:35 *And some of them of understanding shall fall, to try them, and to purge, and to make them white, even to the time of the end: because it is yet for a time appointed.*

Remember that "one foot in the past one foot in the present" thing? This is another good example. During the battle, a lot of good men died. We think that good people should not suffer or die, but they do. This is a sinful world; it is to be expected. But that will be especially true in the last days. The phrase *time of the end* that you see in this verse is a clear reference to the last days, especially the Tribulation Period. The nation of Israel, especially, will be tried and purged during that time. They will come out of that Great Tribulation recognizing their Messiah, loving and serving Him, but countless good people will have already died while they were in the process of being purged and made white.

But let's go back to the past, to the counter-punch just for a second. In spite of all his power, in spite of the odds, a group of heroes risked it all to do right and defeat evil. Antiochus never believed it could happen, but it did. He was so upset at his defeat to this motley little band of soldiers that he literally starved to death grieving about it.

The Climax of Perversity

Focus in on the last part of verse thirty-five before we get into verse thirty-six. That phrase *time of the end* is important. That lets us know that most of what we will see from here on out is more about the Tribulation Period than it is about the trials under Antiochus Epiphanes. Antiochus should be fading from your vision right now, and Antichrist should be coming into focus.

Daniel 11:36 *And the king shall do according to his will; and he shall exalt himself, and magnify himself above every god, and shall speak marvellous things against the God of gods, and shall prosper till the indignation be accomplished: for that that is determined shall be done.*

The first thing you notice about Antichrist is that he *shall do according to his will.* Antichrist is all about Antichrist. He will not be willing to answer to any man on earth. He will be an absolute dictator. Antichrist will *exalt himself,* and *magnify himself above every god.* Even Antiochus did not do that, he set up an altar to Jupiter. Antichrist will proclaim himself as god. And then as the last part of the verse says, he will *speak marvelous things against the God of gods.* In other words, he will say things against God that will make even the jaws of the worst sinners drop to the floor. He will succeed in what he does till the very end of the indignation, the end of the Tribulation Period when Jesus comes and cleans his clock. That is what the verse means when it says *for that that is determined shall be done.* Antichrist will lose, God has already decided it!

Daniel 11:37 *Neither shall he regard the God of his fathers, nor the desire of women, nor regard any god: for he shall magnify himself above all.*

There are two more bits of information we can glean about Antichrist from this verse. We already know that he will not serve God, choosing instead to magnify himself over God. But from this verse we also learn that he *will not regard the God of his fathers.* We do not know what god that was, but his forefathers will have had some form of religion. Antichrist will

209

not only hate and defy the one true God; he will also hate and defy the false gods of his fathers.

The second thing we learn from this verse is that he will not regard *the desire of women*. The word *regard* in this verse means to understand. Simply put, Antichrist will not understand what is so desirable about women and why men like them. He will be a sodomite, a pervert. This ought to tell you how close we probably are to the coming of Christ and the Tribulation Period. We are for the first time ever living in a day when being a sodomite will not keep a man from becoming the leader of the entire world.

Daniel 11:38 *But in his estate shall he honour the God of forces: and a god whom his fathers knew not shall he honour with gold, and silver, and with precious stones, and pleasant things.*

Remember that according to verse thirty-seven, Antichrist will not regard any god. That may make verse thirty-eight confusing when it says he will *honor the God of forces*. But when you look at the definition of "forces" it will make perfect sense. It basically means "strength and power." Now let me show you another verse:

Isaiah 14:14 *I will ascend above the heights of the clouds; I will be like the most High.*

That is the devil talking, the boss of the Antichrist. When he tried to overthrow God, he said, "I will be like El Elyon." I will be like the Strongest Strong One, I will be like the Most High." The devil has never been interested in being merciful like God, or loving like God, or gracious like God. The only attribute of God that the devil has ever been interested in is His power. The devil regards himself as "the god of power, the god of forces."

Antichrist will forsake the true God, he will forsake every false god that his fathers ever worshiped, and he will worship the devil himself with gold, silver, jewels, and all manner of precious things. You may think, "But I thought he would proclaim himself as God." Exactly right. He will be the second member of the satanic trinity, just like Jesus is the

210

second member of the Divine Trinity. This will be blasphemy of the highest order.

Daniel 11:39 *Thus shall he do in the most strong holds with a strange god, whom he shall acknowledge and increase with glory: and he shall cause them to rule over many, and shall divide the land for gain.*

This verse bears out what I just said about the last verse. Notice that it does not say that he would cause *him, Satan,* to rule over many, it says he would cause *them, Satan and Antichrist* to rule over many.

Daniel 11:40 *And at the time of the end shall the king of the south push at him: and the king of the north shall come against him like a whirlwind, with chariots, and with horsemen, and with many ships; and he shall enter into the countries, and shall overflow and pass over.*

Here again we see that this is at *the time of the end*, the last days. For a little bit of further proof, let me remind you that Antiochus in his day was the king of the north. But in this verse the person being spoken of is going to be pushed at by both the king of the north and the king of the south. Antichrist's kingdom according to repeated prophecies in Daniel is made of iron and clay mixed, it is fractured, and at the very end of it, part of his own world-wide empire will turn against him, including Egypt and Syria.

Daniel 11:41 *He shall enter also into the glorious land, and many countries shall be overthrown: but these shall escape out of his hand, even Edom, and Moab, and the chief of the children of Ammon.*

Antichrist will be like Antiochus in that he will have an intense hatred for the Jews and Israel. He will enter into that glorious land to wreak havoc. But at least three countries in this verse will escape out of his hand: Edom, Moab, and the chief of the children of Ammon. Three of the Arab states, made up of descendants of these three ancient enemies of Israel, will be able to hold out against Antichrist. They will find out that he was not their friend after all. He will sucker them in by hating the Jews just like they do, and they will not realize till late in the game that he hates them as well.

Daniel 11:42 *He shall stretch forth his hand also upon the countries: and the land of Egypt shall not escape.* *43 But he shall have power over the treasures of gold and of silver, and over all the precious things of Egypt: and the Libyans and the Ethiopians shall be at his steps.*

Aided by the Libyans and Ethiopians, Antichrist will overrun Egypt and gain control of her vast wealth.

Daniel 11:44 *But tidings out of the east and out of the north shall trouble him: therefore he shall go forth with great fury to destroy, and utterly to make away many.*

North and east of the glorious land is a good description of Iran and Russia. That kind of an alliance would indeed trouble Antichrist. And not one to like being rebelled against, he is going to be in a killing mood when this happens. No wonder that one of the four horsemen of the apocalypse in Revelation 6:4 is the red horse of war. *Make away many* basically means "to make them go away." As in "six feet under, pushing up daisies, assuming room temperature, becoming a subterranean salad bar, dead." Antichrist will be a lethal killer!

Daniel 11:45 *And he shall plant the tabernacles of his palace between the seas in the glorious holy mountain; yet he shall come to his end, and none shall help him.*

Between the Mediterranean Sea and the Dead Sea, on Mount Zion itself, Antichrist will put up his tabernacle, wave his banner, and sing his own praises. He will be as bad as bad can be. Empowered by Satan, he will be more wicked and vile and deadly than any man that has ever lived. He will for a time rule the entire earth and be so powerful that he is not afraid to shake his fist at Heaven and curse God to his face. But did you notice the end of this verse? This chapter could not end any better:

...yet he shall come to his end, and none shall help him.

Jesus is going to come from Heaven on that white horse, the armies of Heaven riding behind him, and with the

212

spoken word from the King of Kings, the reign of Antichrist is over, and he goes from hero to zero, from hill to Hell, from the spire to the fire.

Once again, let's see some practical applications in closing. One, choose your leaders wisely. The decision that Mathias made turned the tide and led to the overthrow of Antiochus. Two, you do right and let others name you. So many are concerned about "labeling themselves" in some great way. Judas Maccabee just did right, and others gave him the name of Hammer! Three, be looking for Jesus to come back soon. We are living in a day when the world will not have any problem following the Antichrist, even though he is a pervert. The time is right for the trumpet to sound!

Chapter 17
Such as Never Was

Daniel 12:1 *And at that time shall Michael stand up, the great prince which standeth for the children of thy people: and there shall be a time of trouble, such as never was since there was a nation even to that same time: and at that time thy people shall be delivered, every one that shall be found written in the book. 2 And many of them that sleep in the dust of the earth shall awake, some to everlasting life, and some to shame and everlasting contempt. 3 And they that be wise shall shine as the brightness of the firmament; and they that turn many to righteousness as the stars for ever and ever. 4 But thou, O Daniel, shut up the words, and seal the book, even to the time of the end: many shall run to and fro, and knowledge shall be increased. 5 Then I Daniel looked, and, behold, there stood other two, the one on this side of the bank of the river, and the other on that side of the bank of the river. 6 And one said to the man clothed in linen, which was upon the waters of the river, How long shall it be to the end of these wonders? 7 And I heard the man clothed in linen, which was upon the waters of the river, when he held up his right hand and his left hand unto heaven, and sware by him that liveth for ever that it shall be for a time, times, and an half; and when he shall have accomplished to scatter the power of the holy people, all these things shall be finished. 8 And I heard, but I understood not:*

then said I, O my Lord, what shall be the end of these things?
9 *And he said, Go thy way, Daniel: for the words are closed up and sealed till the time of the end.* **10** *Many shall be purified, and made white, and tried; but the wicked shall do wickedly: and none of the wicked shall understand; but the wise shall understand.* **11** *And from the time that the daily sacrifice shall be taken away, and the abomination that maketh desolate set up, there shall be a thousand two hundred and ninety days.* **12** *Blessed is he that waiteth, and cometh to the thousand three hundred and five and thirty days.* **13** *But go thou thy way till the end be: for thou shalt rest, and stand in thy lot at the end of the days.*

This is it, the last chapter of the book of Daniel. We have seen Jerusalem fall, Daniel and his friends taken into captivity, four teenage boys purpose not to defile themselves, Daniel interpreting the dream of Nebuchadnezzar, and three Hebrew boys cast into the fire where God met them and kept them safe. We saw Nebuchadnezzar brought down to the level of a beast, and then we saw the handwriting on the wall. Daniel found himself cast into the lions' den, and then received one vision after another of the last days. Chapters seven through eleven have shown us incredible detail from history, but remember that it was prophecy when Daniel wrote it.

Chapter eleven has been unique even by the standards of this very unique book. We took four chapters to look at the details of what happened when the kingdom of Alexander the Great was divided into four parts, and especially saw a lot of details about Egypt and Syria and all of the Antiochuses and Ptolemys that ruled over them and fought against each other. We got to see a couple of feisty females that changed history, Bernice and Cleopatra. And in the last part of the chapter we examined in detail that wicked man from the past, Antiochus Epiphanes and his anti-type yet to come, the Antichrist.

We worked our way all the way up until the time yet to come when Antichrist will proclaim himself as god, specifically as the second member of the satanic trinity. And that is where the narrative picks up in chapter twelve.

A Champion Rises

Daniel 12:1 *And at that time shall Michael stand up, the great prince which standeth for the children of thy people: and there shall be a time of trouble, such as never was since there was a nation even to that same time: and at that time thy people shall be delivered, every one that shall be found written in the book.*

This verse ties in with something we find in the book of the Revelation. When we compare what we see in Revelation 12 with what is here in Daniel 12, an amazing picture comes into view:

Revelation 12:7 *And there was war in heaven: Michael and his angels fought against the dragon; and the dragon fought and his angels,* **8** *And prevailed not; neither was their place found any more in heaven.* **9** *And the great dragon was cast out, that old serpent, called the Devil, and Satan, which deceiveth the whole world: he was cast out into the earth, and his angels were cast out with him.*

During the Tribulation Period, Lucifer, Satan, will make another attempt to overthrow God. Just imagine this, let your mind wrap around it. 6,000 years before this time the devil was an unsatisfied angel, lifted up in pride. He led a rebellion against God and lost. For 6,000 years he has been merely an occasional, invited, enemy guest in Heaven. He has been allowed access into Heaven just to give account of himself and accuse the brethren. But there will come a day, not too long from now, when the devil gathers his forces again. For all these centuries, there have been demons running around everywhere, doing insignificant little things. They have been pushing pornography, brewing beer, causing men to lust after other men, and women to lust after women. They have been stirring up gossip and working to split churches and giving clothing designers ideas for more and more immodest clothing as the years go by. These things are so huge to us but so insignificant by their standards. They have simply been biding their time, waiting for the summons to come from their leader, the devil. They have been gnashing their teeth for another all out assault on the throne room of God, and at the mid-way point of the Tribulation Period, when the devil's Antichrist is at the height of his power, the call for the assault will come. Demonic wings will drone, sulfurous breath will fill the air, satanic screams will pierce the ears, and untold millions of fallen angels will rocket towards Heaven.

Their coming will be expected. Michael the archangel, Michael who used to be second in command to Lucifer among the ranks of angels, Michael whom God has assigned to stand up for the children of Israel, will be waiting at the gates. Behind him will be stretched out all of the ranks of the un-fallen angels.

This is fascinating to consider: if He wanted to, God could simply speak the word, the devil would be defeated, and there would not have to be a fight in Heaven. But God will actually let this battle take place. He will allow war to take place in Heaven. Angels and demons will collide. Wings and talons will be severed. There will be screaming, rage, swords clashing, flashes of light, black clouds of sulfur. Somewhere through it all, you know that the two commanders will meet. Imagine when Michael and Satan spin to face their next opponent... and find themselves staring at each other. They used to worship God together. They used to be so close. And now they find themselves on totally opposite sides, Michael leading the forces of light, and Satan leading the forces of darkness. Imagine the power, the very ground of Heaven shaking as their swords meet. There has never, ever, been a battle like this one. Maybe everything around them continues to rage, but I doubt it. I have to believe that when these two finally meet, everyone around them steps back to watch...

This battle marks the half way point of the Tribulation Period. After Satan is defeated here, he will turn his full wrath loose on earth, especially on Israel. No wonder God said that this would be for Israel *a time of trouble, such as never was since there was a nation* **(Israel)** *even to that same time:*

For such a time as that, God allows the very best of the best of the angelic ranks, Michael the archangel, to rise and fight. He then makes a note that *at that time thy people shall be delivered, every one that shall be found written in the book.*

Those of Israel who receive Christ during that awful time and have their names written in the book will be delivered. Just as he promised in Isaiah 1:27, God is going to redeem Zion, His people, with judgment.

A Call to Resurrection

Daniel 12:2 *And many of them that sleep in the dust of the earth shall awake, some to everlasting life, and some to shame and everlasting contempt.*

Daniel has been told about so much death. Good people dying, bad people dying, death ruling all around. But this verse introduces something that the New Testament would later expound upon greatly: those people that die, good and bad, are not going to stay dead. Their bodies, no matter what condition they have decomposed into, will be brought back together, re-united with their souls, and they will stand before God.

Two different and distinct resurrections are mentioned in this verse: the resurrection to everlasting life and the resurrection to everlasting contempt. In other words, the resurrection of the saved and the resurrection of the lost. But there were two things that Daniel was not told here about these two resurrections, things that we learn from the New Testament. First of all, he was not told that the resurrection of the saved would be in two parts. The first part will be at the Rapture, which happens just before the Tribulation Period begins, and the second part will be at the end of the Tribulation Period for those who accepted Christ during that awful time and lost their lives because of it.

The second thing he was not told was that there would be a thousand plus year gap between the resurrection of the saved and the resurrection of the lost. The wicked dead will not be resurrected till the end of the Millennial Reign of Christ. But mark this down, people from the cults who tell you that when you are dead you are done are just dead wrong! Saved

219

or lost, you will be resurrected, and you will stand before God either at the Judgment Seat of Christ for the saved or at the Great White Throne Judgment for the lost.

Two resurrections – but let me show you which one is more important to God:

Daniel 12:3 *And they that be wise shall shine as the brightness of the firmament; and they that turn many to righteousness as the stars for ever and ever.*

That is referring back to the resurrection of the saved, those who will stand before the Judgement Seat of Christ. We may be beaten and battered and scarred in this life; but in our resurrection we will be wrinkle-free, spotless and pure, bright and shining, glorified forever with Christ!

A Closed Revelation

As you have heard many times, "Revelation" means "unveiling" or "unsealing." The book of the Revelation opens up for us what we know about the coming Tribulation and the end of days and (from our perspective) the beginning of eternity. In fact, God specifically told John not to seal up what he wrote in the book of the Revelation:

Revelation 22:10 *And he saith unto me, Seal not the sayings of the prophecy of this book: for the time is at hand.*

But when Daniel was given his prophecy of these things to come, God told him to seal it up:

Daniel 12:4a *But thou, O Daniel, shut up the words, and seal the book...*

In other words, when Daniel picked up his pen from the parchment, he closed it up, and God closed up any detailed understanding of it. Even as the book of Daniel was later opened and copied and distributed, no one could really get a grip on what it meant, especially the details about the last days. No one would really be able to grasp the end time prophecies until the last days. Do you know what that tells us? We are now in the last days! We can read the book of the Revelation that reveals what Daniel had sealed, and we can then look at our own world in our own day and see what both Daniel in the book of Daniel and John in the book of the Revelation wrote about!

Maybe you for some reason are not convinced of that. If that is the case, the last half of this verse may help to convince you:

Daniel 12:4 *But thou, O Daniel, shut up the words, and seal the book, **even to the time of the end: many shall run to and fro, and knowledge shall be increased.***

That is the description of what things would be like during the last days when these things would come to pass. Many shall run to and fro and knowledge shall increase. Are we there? Go back a hundred years or so. People were riding on horseback at fifteen to twenty miles per hour, which was about as fast as people had been traveling for all 5,900 years before it. In the last hundred years everything changed. We now have cars, trains, power boats, and huge airplanes that carry people seven miles up in the sky for thousands of miles in just a couple of hours. For 5,900 years, people looked up at the moon from the earth. In the last 50 years, man has looked down at the earth from the moon. People are, like never ever before, *running to and fro.* You most likely traveled more miles in the last two weeks than the average person did in an entire lifetime up until 100 years ago.

Are we in the days when *knowledge has increased?*

For the first 5,900 years of human history, knowledge crept along little by little at a snail's pace. The last 100 years or so has seen a greater increase in human knowledge than the entire 5,900 previous years combined. The last 100 or so years have given us the computer, the space shuttle, the electron microscope, the mapping of human DNA, micro-biology, the international space station, the artificial heart, cloning, nuclear physics, cell phones, television, radio, colleges by the tens of thousands, hand-held electronic translators, laser eye surgery, chemotherapy, hyper baric chambers, GPS navigation, I could go on and on. Yes, we are living in the exact days that God described to Daniel as the last days! We are living in the days when the closed revelation of Daniel has been opened wide for us to see and understand.

A Climactic Rebellion

Daniel 12:5 *Then I Daniel looked, and, behold, there stood other two, the one on this side of the bank of the river, and the other on that side of the bank of the river. 6 And one said to the man clothed in linen, which was upon the waters of the river, How long shall it be to the end of these wonders? 7 And I heard the man clothed in linen, which was upon the waters of the river, when he held up his right hand and his left hand unto heaven, and sware by him that liveth for ever that it shall be for a time, times, and an half; and when he shall have accomplished to scatter the power of the holy people, all these things shall be finished.*

Daniel is now seeing three angels instead of one. He has been talking to one angel who has been right over the very middle of the Tigris River talking to him. I am sure that is not anything impressive to an angel, but how amazing would that be to get to see that as a human, an angel hovering over a river talking to you?

Now Daniel is seeing two more to go along with the first. There is the angel over the river, and one on either side of the river. One of those angels asked the first one how long all of this would last, specifically the part about the time of trouble *such as never was* that verse one spoke of. The answer the angel returned was *a time, times, and an half.* And I love the mannerisms used as he answered. This angel held up both hands to Heaven, placed all of the authority for the pronouncement upon God Himself, and gave the answer. Do not ever let anyone tell you not to be expressive! If it is acceptable for an angel to raise his hands, it is surely acceptable for us as well!

Revelation 12:14 uses the exact same terminology of time, times, and half a time to describe this. Three and a half years is what it means. The awful time *such as never was* will last for three and a half years.

Daniel 12:8 *And I heard, but I understood not: then said I, O my Lord, what shall be the end of these things?* **9** *And he said, Go thy way, Daniel: for the words are closed up and sealed till the time of the end.*

This is another instance of the fact that the prophets were inspired to write the exact words of God, but they themselves often did not understand the meaning of what they were writing. Daniel did not understand all of the details or even the duration of what was going to happen, so he asked for further clarification. He did not get it.

The angel told him in so many words: Go on about you business, you don't really need to know, what you have had revealed to you is for others to understand much much later.

Daniel 12:10 *Many shall be purified, and made white, and tried; but the wicked shall do wickedly: and none of the wicked shall understand; but the wise shall understand.*

The words were sealed to Daniel, but a few more details for us to understand were given. From this verse, we learn that those who get saved during the Tribulation Period will be *purified, and made white, and tried.* Those are three terms that let us know they are going to go through the worst trials imaginable. The Christians facing lions in the Roman Coliseum and being covered in tar and burned as torches in Nero's garden had it bad, but not nearly as bad as Tribulation saints will have it. You would think that they would be whining, "We just don't understand!" But on the contrary, look again at the last part of verse ten:

...but the wicked shall do wickedly: and none of the wicked shall understand; but the wise shall understand.

The vast majority of the world during the Tribulation Period will be lost, living like the devil, on their way to Hell as fast as they can go, and not one of them will understand it! But the saved, the wise, they will understand it all, and they will with perfect understanding gladly lay down their lives for Christ.

Daniel 12:11 *And from the time that the daily sacrifice shall be taken away, and the abomination that maketh desolate*

set up, there shall be a thousand two hundred and ninety days.
12 Blessed is he that waiteth, and cometh to the thousand three
hundred and five and thirty days.

Two more time periods are given in these two verses.
We already saw in verse seven a time frame of 1,260 days,
three and a half Biblical years of 360 days each. In verse
eleven, we see a time period of 1,290 days, thirty more days
than the last half of the Tribulation Period. Why the extra thirty
days? I think a pretty good answer is found in Matthew 25:31-
46:

Matthew 25:31 *When the Son of man shall come in his*
glory, and all the holy angels with him, then shall he sit upon
the throne of his glory: 32 And before him shall be gathered
all nations: and he shall separate them one from another, as a
shepherd divideth his sheep from the goats: 33 And he shall set
the sheep on his right hand, but the goats on the left. 34 Then
shall the King say unto them on his right hand, Come, ye
blessed of my Father, inherit the kingdom prepared for you
from the foundation of the world: 35 For I was an hungred,
and ye gave me meat: I was thirsty, and ye gave me drink: I
was a stranger, and ye took me in: 36 Naked, and ye clothed
me: I was sick, and ye visited me: I was in prison, and ye came
unto me. 37 Then shall the righteous answer him, saying, Lord,
when saw we thee an hungred, and fed thee? or thirsty, and
gave thee drink? 38 When saw we thee a stranger, and took
thee in? or naked, and clothed thee? 39 Or when saw we thee
sick, or in prison, and came unto thee? 40 And the King shall
answer and say unto them, Verily I say unto you, Inasmuch as
ye have done it unto one of the least of these my brethren, ye
have done it unto me. 41 Then shall he say also unto them on
the left hand, Depart from me, ye cursed, into everlasting fire,
prepared for the devil and his angels: 42 For I was an hungred,
and ye gave me no meat: I was thirsty, and ye gave me no
drink: 43 I was a stranger, and ye took me not in: naked, and
ye clothed me not: sick, and in prison, and ye visited me not.
44 Then shall they also answer him, saying, Lord, when saw
we thee an hungred, or athirst, or a stranger, or naked, or sick,

or in prison, and did not minister unto thee? **45** *Then shall he answer them, saying, Verily I say unto you, Inasmuch as ye did it not to one of the least of these, ye did it not to me.* **46** *And these shall go away into everlasting punishment: but the righteous into life eternal.*

Notice that this is a judgment not of individuals, but of entire nations! During some point of the Tribulation Period, entire nations will either accept God and help His people Israel, or reject God and not help His people. Those nations will be assembled before God to answer for what they have done, and there surely has to be a time period to allow that to happen.

The second time period mentioned in verse twelve is 1,335 days, forty-five more days after the additional 30. We are given a pretty good clue I think as to what that time period is about as well. We know that according to Revelation 20:4 that during the Millennial Reign of Christ, we will rule and reign with Him. That would take a little while to set up as well and fits perfectly with what would likely happen after the judgment of the nations. A time period of forty-five days seems about right for all of that to be set into place, and it surely would match the description of a "blessing" that verse twelve gives.[15]

A Calming Reassurance

Daniel 12:13 *But go thou thy way till the end be: for thou shalt rest, and stand in thy lot at the end of the days.*

Don't you know that hearing of all of this trouble, a time that for the Jews will be *such as never was*, had to tear Daniel up inside? God surely knew that. And our gracious God, ever concerned about a dear old servant like Daniel, was not going to let things end for him on that kind of note. Rest was coming for Daniel. Soon he would REALLY be home...

And there was coming a day when Daniel would not just get to see the fulfillment of these end time prophecies, he would have a part in it! Daniel will "stand in his lot at the end of the days." I do not know what "lot" that is, but I suspect it is somewhere very near to the throne.

Notes

1. "Nebuchadnezzar," #4 Political History, International Standard Bible Encyclopedia, 1952

2. Adam Clarke, Clarke's Commentary, 6 vols. (New York: Abingdon-Cokesbury Press) 4:584-585

3. N. W. Hutchings, Exploring the Book of Daniel, (Oklahoma City: Hearthstone Publishing, 1990), 119-120

4. Jamison, Fausset, Brown, A Commentary of the Old and New Testament, 3 vols. (Peabody, MA: Hendrickson Publsihers) 2:410-412

5. Adam Clarke, Clarke's Commentary, 6 vols. (New York: Abingdon-Cokesbury Press) 4:593

6. Jamison, Fausset, Brown, A Commentary of the Old and New Testament, 3 vols. (Peabody, MA: Hendrickson Publsihers) 2:426

7. Matthew Henry, Commentary on the Whole Bible, 6 vols. (New York: Fleming H. Revell Company) 4:1078

8. H. L. Willmington, Willmington's Guide to the Bible, 2 vols. (Wheaton, IL: Tyndale House Publishers, Inc., 1986) 1:236

9. Jamison, Fausset, Brown, A Commentary of the Old and New Testament, 3 vols. (Peabody, MA: Hendrickson Publsihers) 2:434

10. H. L. Willmington, <u>Willmington's Guide to the Bible</u>, 2 vols. (Wheaton, IL: Tyndale House Publishers, Inc., 1986) 1:238

11. Matthew Henry, <u>Commentary on the Whole Bible</u>, 6 vols. (New York: Fleming H. Revell Company) 4:1078

12. Adam Clarke, <u>Clarke's Commentary</u>, 6 vols. (New York: Abingdon-Cokesbury Press) 4:610

13. Adam Clarke, <u>Clarke's Commentary</u>, 6 vols. (New York: Abingdon-Cokesbury Press) 4:611

14. Adam Clarke, <u>Clarke's Commentary</u>, 6 vols. (New York: Abingdon-Cokesbury Press) 4:612

15. H. L. Willmington, <u>Willmington's Guide to the Bible</u>, 2 vols. (Wheaton, IL: Tyndale House Publishers, Inc., 1986) 1:243

22000252R00123

Made in the USA
Charleston, SC
10 September 2013